Vedic Astrology

The Ultimate Guide to Hindu Astrology and the 12 Zodiac Signs

© Copyright 2020

The contents of this book may not be reproduced, duplicated or transmitted without direct written permission from the author.

Under no circumstances will any legal responsibility or blame be held against the publisher for any reparation, damages, or monetary loss due to the information herein, either directly or indirectly.

Legal Notice:

This book is copyright protected. This is only for personal use. You cannot amend, distribute, sell, use, quote or paraphrase any part or the content within this book without the consent of the author.

Disclaimer Notice:

Please note the information contained within this document is for educational and entertainment purposes only. Every attempt has been made to provide accurate, up to date and reliable complete information. No warranties of any kind are expressed or implied. Readers acknowledge that the author is not engaging in the rendering of legal, financial, medical or professional advice. The content of this book has been derived from various sources. Please consult a licensed professional before attempting any techniques outlined in this book.

By reading this document, the reader agrees that under no circumstances is the author responsible for any losses, direct or indirect, which are incurred as a result of the use of information contained within this document, including, but not limited to, errors, omissions, or inaccuracies.

Your Free Gift (only available for a limited time)

Thanks for getting this book! If you want to learn more about various spirituality topics, then join Mari Silva's community and get a free guided meditation MP3 for awakening your third eye. This guided meditation mp3 is designed to open and strengthen ones third eye so you can experience a higher state of consciousness. Simply visit the link below the image to get started.

https://spiritualityspot.com/meditation

Contents

INTRODUCTION 1
CHAPTER 1: INTRODUCTION TO ANCIENT VEDIC ASTROLOGICAL TEXTS 3
    History of Vedic Astrology 4
    Ancient Classical Texts of Vedic Astrology 6
    Branches of Vedic Astrology 11
CHAPTER 2: THE STELLAR KINGDOM: THE STORY OF THE NINE PLANETS 13
CHAPTER 3: PLANETARY INFLUENCES ON DAILY LIFE 33
    Five-Fold Relationship 33
    Natural Friends and Enemies of Rahu and Ketu 39
    Reciprocal and Non-Reciprocal Friendships, Enmity, and Relationships 41
CHAPTER 4: HOUSE SYSTEMS AND CHARACTERISTICS OF BHAVA 45
    The 12 Houses or Bhavas 46
    Interesting Points about the Various Houses 55
    Understanding Bhavatah Bhava 56
CHAPTER 5: SIDDHANT SHASTRA: MATHEMATICAL AND ASTRONOMICAL PRINCIPLES 58
    Understanding Ayanamsa 59
    Understanding Dasas 62

CHAPTER 6: THE FIRST FOUR: ARIES, TAURUS, GEMINI, AND CANCER 66
- Categories by Flexibility 68
- Categories by Elements 68
- Categories by Gender 69
- Other Significant Categorizations 70
- Aries - Mesha Rashi 70
- Taurus - Vrishabha Rashi 71
- Gemini - Mithuna Rashi 72
- Cancer - Karka Rashi 73

CHAPTER 7: THE MIDDLE EARTH: LEO, VIRGO, LIBRA, AND SCORPIO 75
- Leo - Simha Rashi 75
- Virgo - Kanya Rashi 76
- Libra - Tula Rashi 78
- Scorpio - Vrishchika Rashi 79

CHAPTER 8: THE HEAVEN ABOVE: SAGITTARIUS, CAPRICORN, AQUARIUS, AND PISCES 81
- Sagittarius - Dhanush Rashi 81
- Capricorn - Makar Rashi 83
- Aquarius - Kumbh Rashi 84
- Pisces - Meena Rashi 85

CHAPTER 9: DIVISIONAL CHARTS 87
- Implication and Importance of Divisional Charts 92

CHAPTER 10: PLANETARY STRENGTHS AND AVASTHAS 95
- Significance of Residential Strength of a Planet 97
- Significance of Nakshatra Placement 97
- Significance of Planetary Strengths in Varga Charts 98
- Shadbala - The Six-Fold Strength in Vedic Astrology 100
- Dik Bala - the Directional Strength 102
- Kala Bala - the Time Strength 103
- Chesta Bala - Strength from the Motion of Planets 104
- Naisargika Bala - the Natural Strength 105
- Drgbala - the Aspect Strength 106

CHAPTER 11: TIMING OF EVENTS: DASHAS AND TRANSITS..............108
  CASE STUDY I.. 109
  TRANSIT OF PLANETS 111
CHAPTER 12: ASHTAKAVARGA: DESTINY DOTS AT A GLANCE........114
  HOW TO USE THE ASHTAKAVARGA TABLE FOR RASHI CHART
  INTERPRETATION 116
  CASE STUDY OF ASHTAKAVARGA TABLE SCORES 118
CONCLUSION..120
HERE'S ANOTHER BOOK BY MARI SILVA THAT YOU MIGHT LIKE 121
YOUR FREE GIFT (ONLY AVAILABLE FOR A LIMITED TIME) 122
RESOURCES 123

Introduction

Vedic Astrology or Jyotishya is a gift to the world from ancient India, predating the Christian era. This science is not experimentally contrived but perceived through the power of enlightened vision by ancient sages and seers, notably among them, Sage Parashara, believed to be the original author of the Vedic texts.

Vedic Astrology is the need of the hour considering the confusing milieu that boggles the modern world. Despite the apparent achievement of high levels of modern materialistic comfort, we are still doggedly pursuing sustainable happiness. The primary reason for this dichotomy is that we don't seem to know or accept that each of us is unique and has different needs and life purposes.

Vedic Astrology is a tool of wisdom gifted to us by the ancient seers of India to help us understand this uniqueness of our individuality so we can follow the path of our personal life purpose.

This book is written with the view of teaching the basics of Vedic Astrology to the beginner. And yet, people who already have a reasonably sound knowledge of this fascinating and vast subject will benefit from it. The book contains numerous aspects of Vedic Astrology within its covers. Knowing you can access a wide variety of topics without having to shift from one book to another is a great advantage for both new and experienced learners.

Starting from the most basic part, namely a simple yet powerful introduction to this ancient but timeless subject - right up to the complex and layered topic of Ashtakavarga tables, this book is great for all those interested in Vedic Astrology. Furthermore, this book is up-to-date and comprehensive, giving both beginners and experts the perfect combination to learn and refresh their knowledge on the various subtopics of Jyotishya.

A beginner can start from Chapter 1 and learn step-by-step as the complexity increases. An expert could just flip through the table of contents and choose a topic he or she needs to access immediately and clear any doubt arising at the moment. Therefore, although it is a beginner book, it can be a valuable addition for an expert too.

Chapter 1: Introduction to Ancient Vedic Astrological Texts

Centuries ago, India's ancient sages and rishis had spoken about the now-popular concept of self-awareness, which is proven to be highly beneficial for the growth and development of an individual. The ancient seers said, "Self-knowledge is the basis of all knowledge." The more you know about yourself, the better your ability to assimilate external knowledge learned from books, teachers, guides, and mentors.

Learning about yourself includes knowing the effects of the planetary system on your life, which is what Vedic Astrology or Jyotishya is about. Jyotish, in Sanskrit, translates as "the science of light." It is an important limb of the Vedas, the ancient sacred texts of India, and the Sanatana Dharma, which the western world knows as Hinduism. Jyotish is referred to with other names and different spellings, including:

- Jyotisha
- Jyotishya
- Hindu Astrology
- Vedic Astrology

- Indian Astrology

The term *Hindu Astrology* has been in use since the beginning of the 19th century. Vedic Astrology gained prominence, especially in the western world, around the 1970s, thanks to Yoga and Ayurveda's spread. Vedanga Jyotishya is one of the earliest astronomical texts found within the Vedas, dated many centuries before Christ's birth.

Vedic Astrology is based on two primary concepts in Hinduism, namely karma and rebirth. Simplistically put, in Hinduism, the law of Karma states we live and work within certain parameters and limitations created by actions or karma performed in our previous lifetimes. Therefore, it is possible to predict our future through Vedic Astrology, which has the power to demonstrate which of the previous karma will come to fruition in the present lifetime.

And it paves the path to spiritual development by showing how individuals can improve their quality of life through the practice of higher thoughts and better living.

History of Vedic Astrology

There are six Vedangas, the auxiliary disciplines of the Indian Vedic System of learning. These six Vedangas or branches of studies are essential for the support of Vedic rituals and education. They are:

- Shiksha (Phonetics)
- Kalpa (Ritual Canon)
- Vyakaran (Grammar)
- Nirukta (Explanation)
- Chhanda (Vedic Meter)
- Jyotishya (Astrology)

Vedanga Jyotishya is one of the earliest known texts on Vedic Astrology. The extant work is dated to the last few centuries B.C. But it is strongly believed that the Vedanga Jyotishya describes a tradition that goes back at least to 600-700 B.C.

The Vedanga Jyotishya is highly relevant to the dating of the Vedas because it depicts the winter solstice for the period around 1400 B.C. This story of the winter solstice is used to discover the antiquity of the Vedas. There are two versions of the Vedanga Jyotishya, one for the Rig Veda and a second one for the Yajur Veda. Both these recensions have the same verses except for eight extra verses in the Yajur Veda recension.

Experts believe that the description of the winter solstice around 1400 B.C. means the text was written around the same time. Other experts felt this period's narrative does not mean it was written then because it could have been recorded later. Regardless of its antiquity, Vedanga Jyotishya being a significant auxiliary discipline to the study of the Vedas, reflect the criticality of Vedic Astrology in Sanatana Dharma.

The ancient practice of Jyotishya was an important aspect of Vedic rituals, especially to determine the auspicious time and date of yogic events for optimal benefits for all concerned. In multiple Hindu scriptures like the Chandogya Upanishad and the Atharva Veda, there are warnings of demonic eclipses we should be cautious of and do the preparation needed for protection against their negative influence. Chandogya Upanishad talks of Rahu being a "shadowy" figure responsible for eclipse occurrences, an accurate analogical explanation of eclipses, according to modern science.

Today, the Sanskrit word, "*Graha*" means "planet." But "Graha" actually translates to "demon." The foundation of Vedic Astrology lies in the core principle of Sanatana Dharma, which believes there is an infallible connection between the macrocosm and the microcosm. Jyotish is like a lens through which we can gain insight about our lives and understand our extended life, which includes the bigger picture, both in the materialistic and the metaphysical world. What happens to an individual is affected by what happens in the outside world, including the vast astronomical spaces beyond the realm of humans.

Ancient Classical Texts of Vedic Astrology

Many classical texts of Vedic Astrology have been in use from ancient times to the present day. Important names that come to mind when discussing ancient texts are Parashar, Varahamihir, and Jaimini. Let us look at the most important works written by these famous authors and others.

Brihat Parashara Hora Shastra

Believed to have been created by Sage Parashara, a highly learned rishi of the ancient Vedic period, the original version of this large, extant text is supposed to have had 100 chapters. However, no one has the text in its full form. The current form has 13 chapters.

Nearly all scholars agree that the Brihat Parashara Hora Shastra is the most comprehensive and exhaustive compendium on Vedic Astrology. Without studying this, no student can hope to become an effective scholar on the subject. Without it, the student's knowledge will be half-baked, to say the least.

This book contains many important features of Vedic Astrology, including but not limited to:

- Description of planets
- Zodiac signs
- Houses
- Divisional charts

All kinds of mathematical calculations needed for Vedic Astrology students are described in meticulous detail throughout. Another noteworthy feature of this work is the availability of remedial measures for inauspicious births.

Brihat Jatak

This ancient text on Vedic Astrology is believed to have been composed and written by Varahamihira, a famous poet and scholar who was part of the legendary King Vikramaditya, who ruled around 57 B.C. Varahamihira was also a great astronomer.

He was the first one to mention ayanamsa or the shifting of the vernal equinox by exactly 50.32 seconds (which is approximated to 1-degree) every 72 years. This finds mention in Varahamihira's book <u>Pancha Siddhantika</u> based on India's ancient Siddhanta (the Mathematical and Astronomical Branch).

The inclusion of the ayanamsa to arrive at the 12 Zodiac signs of Vedic Astrology is one of the primary differences between Sidereal Astrology (or Vedic Astrology) and Western (or Tropical Astrology) in which this small but impactful shift is not included.

One of the biggest attractions of Brihat Jatak for scholars of Vedic Astrology is the contents of Chapter 10, "Karmajeeva," which deals with the livelihoods of individuals. This important chapter deals with the various earnings that people can have in just four shlokas (or verses). Novices get the feeling that four shlokas are insufficient for an exhaustive repertoire of livelihoods. And yet, the brevity of the chapter speaks volumes on the brilliance of Varahamihira, his immense control over the language, and the subject of Vedic Astrology.

Brihat Samhita

Considered one of the greatest classics of Vedic Astrology, Brihat Samhita was authored by Varahamihira, the same scholar who wrote Brihat Jatak. This text is used to make predictions of nations and kingdoms. It is written in two parts, namely "Pratham Kanda" containing 57 chapters and "Dwitiya Kanda," containing 50 chapters. Varahamihira believed in the importance of having a genuine astrologer for daily life. He also explains how to identify a genuine astrologer from a fake one.

In the Brihat Samhita, there is an entire chapter titled "Vastu Vidya" dedicated to Vastu Shastra (dealing with buildings and architecture), an integral aspect of Vedic Astrology. Many modern astrologers erroneously take Vastu Shastra as being separate from Vedic Astrology. Also, the Brihat Samhita describes in detail how to predict any place's weather and climate.

Ashtakavarga Nibandh

Ashta means "eight" in Sanskrit. Therefore, Ashtakavarga Nibandh means "Eight Vargas." In this book, the ancient rishis of India explain and assess the strength of planets in transit. The ancient Indian seers discovered a unique system through the Ashtakavarga Nibandh, which helps scholars and practitioners of Astrology understand the malignant and beneficial effects of planets on humankind. Based on pure mathematical formulas, the calculation technique used here is unique and not found in any other writing.

Prithyusha, the son of Varahamihira, has said of this book, "The general aspects of planets in transit can be seen or understood elsewhere. However, the finer details can be observed only by using Ashtakavarga." In fact, the Ashtakavarga Nibandh has a mathematical formula that helps to arrive at the longevity of the native (or the individual whose horoscope is being analyzed).

It teaches the astrological practitioner to use the Ashtakavarga in different situations and in different charts, including the birth chart, Horary chart, Divisional chart, Varsha Kundali (or the annual life pattern), and more. Scholars believe there is no content other than Ashtakavarga Nibandh to arrive at an accurate prediction scientifically and mathematically.

Phaladeepika

Phaladeepika is another important passage written by Mantreswara, a prolific author who is believed to have been born in a family of Namboodari Brahmins (a prominent Hindu sect in the southern parts of India) around the 13th century, though some historians believe lived in the 16th century.

The exact dates of his birth and death are not known. At the end of this work, Mantreswara writes that he resided in Shalivati, the present-day district of Tirunelveli of Tamil Nadu, a Southern India state, which is a primary reason for the high popularity of the text in the southern parts of India.

This book deserves to be treated alongside other great ancient works like Brihat Parashara Hora Shastra, Jatak Parijata, Brihat Jataka, etc. This comprehensive work covers nearly all aspects of human life, and its information ranges from the very basic to very advanced.

Saravali

Written by Kalyan Varma, a prolific Sanskrit author of the 10th century, Saravali is treated on par with Brihat Parashar Hora Shastra, Brihat Jataka, and Sarvarth Chintamani. Kalyan Varma was a well-known astrologer and the king of Vyaghrapada believed to be in present-day Madhya Pradesh, a state in Central India. Saravali is an elaborate commentary on all the Vedic Astrology books studied and mastered by Kalyan Varma.

Sarvartha Chintamani

Believed to have been written in the 13th century by Venkatesha Sharma, Sarvartha Chintamani, in Sanskrit, translates to "Gem of Superior Desires and Thoughts." Containing just 17 chapters, it is one of the most popular and most-often cited books on Vedic Astrology. The most important chapters followed closely in this book deal with the yoga-formation of planets and these yogas' outcomes. It also describes the effects of each house in the natal chart, including these elements:

- Description of the planets
- Their effects

- The lifespan of the individual
- Prosperity

This text gives practical and valuable comments relating to placing the 12 houses on an individual's birth chart. It then moves on to describe the astrological explanations on the position of each house and its impacts on the individual. Sarvartha Chintamani also expands Varahamihira's thoughts on the profession of Vedic Astrology.

Jatak Parijaat

This fairly exhaustive work on Vedic Astrology is authored by Sri Vaidyanatha Dikshita, the son of another great scholar, Venkatadri. This work finds a place of honor along with the above three ancient texts and is also prescribed as a textbook for all examinations conducted on Jyotishya. It contains detailed instructions and sections on various essential aspects, including Yogas, Ayurdaya, Ashtakavarga, Vimshottari, Kalachakra Dasha, Stri Jataka, and more. Translated into multiple Indian languages, this monumental book is originally in Sanskrit and is held in high esteem by Indian astrologers all over the country.

Sri Vaidyanatha Dikshita lived in the 15th century and based highly respected work on various ancient texts, including Brihat Parashara Hora Shastra, Brihat Jataka, Saravali, Sarvatha Chintamani, and more. There are 18 chapters in this book covering the entire range of Vedic Astrology, according to the principles of Sage Parashara.

Branches of Vedic Astrology

Three broad categories include:

1. **Siddhanta** - The Siddhanta branch which deals with astronomy and its astrological applications

2. **Samhita** - The branch that handles Mundane Astrology dealing with the prediction of events related to countries. The Samhita branch deals with predicting events like earthquakes, wars, political matters, finances and economics of the country, etc.

3. **Hora** - The Hora (or Predictive) branch is further divided into more branches

The Hora branch is divided into:

- **Jatak Shastra** - Also called Hora Shastra, which deals with predictions based on individual horoscopes or Kundali, the Sanskrit term for horoscope.

- **Muhurat or Muhurtha** - Referred to as Electional Astrology, this branch of Hora Shastra deals with the selection of auspicious and beneficial times for important events for optimal fruition from life activities.

- **Swar Shastra** - Called Phonetical Astrology, this sub-branch deals with predictions based on names and sounds.

- **Prashna Shastra** - Also called Horary Astrology, this sub-branch of Hora Shastra deals with predictions based on the time when the person asks the queries or questions.

- **Ankajyotishya or Kabala** - Called Numerology, this branch deals with predictions based on numbers

- **Nadi Astrology** - This branch works with ancient treatises and texts that have detailed predictions for individuals.

- **Tajik Shastra** - Also called Varsha Phala, this sub-branch of Hora Shastra deals with astrology based on annual solar returns.

- **Jaimini Sutras** - This is a non-conventional branch of Hora Shastra that uses texts written by an ancient Indian astrologer, Acharya Jaimini. He used different but equally accurate astrological methods based on mathematics and astronomy. His works are categorized under a separate branch.

- **Nast jatak** - This branch deals with recovering and/or reconstructing lost horoscopes.

- **Streejatak** - This branch deals exclusively with astrology for female natives.

Now that you have a basic idea of the history and the historical contents of Vedic Astrology, you can learn what has been said about the nine planets and their effects on human life, both collectively and individually.

Chapter 2: The Stellar Kingdom: The Story of the Nine Planets

In Vedic Astrology, the nine heavenly bodies who are worshipped as deities and rule over the 12 zodiac signs are called Navagraha, which translates to "nine planets." The Navagraha or the nine planets include:

- Surya, the Sun
- Chandra, the Moon
- Mangala or Guja, Mars
- Buddha, Mercury
- Brihaspati or Guru, Jupiter
- Shukra, Venus
- Shani, Saturn
- Rahu, the shadow heavenly body (also known as a planet or Graha in Vedic Astrology) associated with the north lunar mode
- Ketu, the shadow planet associated with the south lunar mode

Let us look at each of these nine planets in detail, which is an essential lesson to understand Vedic Astrology.

Surya, the Sun

The Sun or Surya in Sanskrit is the star at the center of our solar system and the largest heavenly body in it. With a diameter of around 1.4 million kilometers, it is primarily made up of hydrogen and helium. Over 99% of the total mass of our solar structure is held by the Sun. The mean distance between the Sun and our planet is about 140 million kilometers. As it is stationary and at the center of our solar system, it never seems retrograde.

The Sun is the king in Vedic Astrology and is considered a royal planet. Surya represents many things, including:

- Our soul
- Willpower
- Paternal relations, especially father, called Pitrukaraka (planet connected with a father)
- The king and other high officials

Surya's color is red, which reflects his hot and angry nature. The metal is gold (like his golden rays), and his gem is ruby. He represents the eastern direction. The Sun stays in each Zodiac sign or Rashi for one month and takes 12 months or one year to complete the full circle of the Zodiac.

The Sun's movement is more or less fixed. Multiple Hindu festivals are celebrated according to the entry of the Sun into the various Rashis. For example, it enters Capricorn or Makar Rashi on January 14th, and this day is celebrated every year as Makar Sankranti. Similarly, on April 13th or 14th, the Sun enters Mesha Rashi or the Aries, and that day is celebrated as Baishakhi or New Year's Day.

Surya in Hindu Mythologyin Hindu Tradition - Surya's story, according to Hindu mythology, is very interesting. His world is known as Suryaloka and is next to the earth or bhumandala. Surya was married to Sanjana, the daughter of the celestial architect, Vishvakarma. Surya and Sanjana had three children: Vaivasvata, Yama, and Yami. Yama is the god of death. There was marital discord between the couple because Sanjana couldn't face her husband's intense heat.

One day, Sanjana left for her father's abode, leaving behind Chaaya (shadow), her body double. After spending time in her father's place, Sanjana left there too. She took on the shape of a mare and went into the mountains to meditate and pray. Surya was unaware of these arrangements made by his wife. He continued to live with Chaaya, and she gave birth to three more children: Savarni, Shani, and Taapti.

One day, Surya came to know of everything. He went in search of Sanjana and found her deep in prayer in the form of a mare. Surya took on the shape of a horse and wooed his wife, which resulted in the birth of the horse-headed twin called Ashwini Kumaras, who became the celestial physicians.

When Sanjana told her husband she couldn't handle the intensity of his heat, he divided his entire power into sixteen parts, which all became heavenly bodies, including the earth. The sun was left with one-sixteenth part of the intensity he originally had, after which Sanjana went back to live with him.

Surya's charioteer's name is Arun, and it was pulled by seven horses whose colors were the same as those in a rainbow. A highly powerful Hindu dynasty known as Suryavanshi is believed to be descendants of the Sun God. The first king of the Suryavanshi Dynasty was Ikshavku. Lord Rama, believed to be an avatar of Lord Vishnu, was born in this divine lineage. Surya, the Sun God, is known by multiple other names, including:

- Ravi, which translates to "praised and worshipped by all".
- Aditya, son of Aditi
- Surya, the supreme light or guide
- Bhanu, a ray of light or the shining one
- Arka, the radiant one
- Bhaskar, the illuminator
- Mitra, everyone's friend
- Marichi, starlight or rays of light
- Sahasranshu, one with thousand rays
- Savita, the one who purifies
- Pushan, the one who nourishes
- Khag, the one who stimulates the senses
- Prabhakar, the crater of shining light
- Martanda, the one who sprung from a lifeless egg
- Chitrabhanu, the lord of flames
- Divakar, the creator of Day
- Hiranyagarbhaya, the one with the golden womb

Important astrological facts about the sun - The temperament of Surya is steady and fixed. His primary quality is Sattva Guna. He belongs to the Kshatriya or Warrior Caste. Surya's nature is malefic and cruel. His strength is displayed when he is in the tenth house of a native's birth chart, and his weak position is when he is in the fourth house.

His natural astrological house is the fifth house. He rules Leo. His exaltation sign is Aries (or Mesha Rashi), and the sign of debilitation is Libra (or Tula Rashi). Surya's friends are Chandra, Guru, and Mangala. His enemies are Shukra and Shani. Sun is neutral with Buddha. The Nakshatras he governs are Krittika, Uttara Phalguni, and Uttarashada.

Positive keywords for Surya are vitality, creativity, confidence, leadership, and generosity. Negative keywords for the Sun are cruelty, arrogance, pomposity, conceit, and aggression. Surya is the controller of the prana or life force and imparts life-giving properties to all our organs. The planet's position in the birth chart plays an important part in the health of the native. Heart problems are primarily due to the affliction of Surya or Leo, the Zodiac sign he rules.

Chandra, the Moon

The Moon is the only natural planet of the earth and the only heavenly body visited by humans. With a diameter of 3475 kilometers and a mean distance of about 380,000 kilometers from earth, the Moon takes the same time (27.3 days) for one revolution around the earth and one rotation about its axis. This is the reason we always get to see only one face of the moon.

The Moon is also a royal planet and is considered the Queen in the hierarchy of Vedic Astrology. Chandra represents emotions, mind, mother, sensitivity, house, and household-related elements, including food and clothing, domestic comforts, sea, and all elements connected to the sea, milk, and the color associated with the Moon, white. She is cool, calm, and represents the north-eastern direction. Her metal is silver, and her gem is pearl.

Chandra is the fastest moving of the Navagrahas and takes about 2 ½ days in each Rashi. When Surya and Chandra are in the same Rashi or Zodiac Sign, it is Amavasya or the New Moon Day, which is also the first day of the dark fortnight. When the Sun and Moon are opposite each other, otherwise known as 180-degrees apart, then it is the Full Moon Day or Purnima, the bright fortnight's first day.

Chandra in Hindu Mythology - Another interesting story is that of the Moon or Chandra. Anasuya was the wife of Sage Atri, a great rishi of ancient times. Anusuya was known for her chastity. One day, the three prominent Hindu Gods, namely Vishnu, Shiva, and Brahma, tested her abstinence. They visited her in disguise and demanded that she feed them her breast milk.

Anusuya saw through the trick and changed the three gods into babies through her divine powers. It was now not a problem feeding the three babies the milk of her breast. The gods were pleased with her behavior and attitude and blessed her to have great sons. Through Vishnu's grace, Anusuya gave birth to Lord Dattatreya. Shiva's blessings resulted in the birth of Sage Durvasa. Lord Brahma's blessings resulted in the birth of the Moon God, Chandra.

Chandra was worshipped by all beings. He married the 27 daughters of Prajapati Daksha, and these 27 daughters became the 27 constellations or Nakshatras in the Zodiac. Interestingly, he preferred to remain with only one of his 27 wives and ignored the other 26 despite them pleading with him to spend time with them all equally.

The 26 daughters complained to their father, Prajapati Daksha, who warned his son-in-law of dire consequences if he is not fair to all his wives. Chandra did not heed his father-in-law's advice, who cursed him to fall ill. Every day, his glow faded, and there seemed to be no remedy for his illness. The gods were alarmed at the effects of life on earth if Chandra died.

So, they approached Daksha and requested him to adjust the curse so life on earth remains unaffected. Daksha agreed to change the curse only after Chandra promised to spend one day each with his 27 wives. With the curse modified, Chandra's would wane for 14 days and regain the glow during the next 14 days, which is the story of the moon's waxing and waning cycle.

Like the Suryavanshi, Chandravanshi was another powerful dynasty that ruled over India. The Chandravanshis believed they were direct descendants of the Moon God. The first king of the Chandravanshi Dynasty was Bharat, the legendary ruler, after whom India gets its Sanskrit name.

Important astrological facts about the moon - The sign in which the Moon is placed during your birth is called Janma Rashi. And the star constellation is your Nakshatra. Moon represents mind and emotion and signifies the mother relationship. Chandra's astrological nature is fickleness and changeability. The element governed by the Moon is water. The primary guna of Chandra is Sattva.

Astrologically, when the moon is waxing, its nature is beneficial. During the waning period, he has a malefic effect. The Moon's strength is felt when he is in the Fourth House, and his power is weak when in the 10th house. The Moon rules over the Zodiac sign, Cancer. Surya and Shukra are his friends, and he has no enemies. Positive elements connected with Chandra are receptivity, sympathy, good memory, and protectiveness. Negative elements relating to Chandra are touchiness, emotional instability, worry, moodiness, and smothering love.

Mangala, Guja, or Mars

Mangala Gruha, Mars is the first planet closest to earth's boundary in space. With a diameter of about 6700 kilometers, this fourth planet in our Solar System takes 687 days for one revolution around the Sign; the period of rotation on its axis is just over 24 hours. It has two natural satellites, namely Phobos and Deimos. The retrograde period of Mangala Gruha ranges between 60-80 days and happens once every 26 months.

Mangala or Guja in Hindu mythology - Once, Prajapati Daksha organized a grand yagna. All the gods and goddesses from all the three worlds were invited for this fabulous yagna. Out of earlier spite, Daksha deliberately left out Lord Shiva, who was also his son-in-law, from the invitation list.

Sati, Lord Shiva's wife, and Daksha's daughter were keen ongoing for the yagna even without an invitation. Lord Shive did not agree and warned her not to go to her father's house. But Sati ignored her husband's warnings and went to her father's abode.

On reaching the place where the yagna was being conducted, Sati was insulted by her insolent, arrogant father, who also made unpleasant remarks about Lord Shiva. Sati was so furious with Daksha she cursed the yagna and all the other invitees who did not find the courage to protest the powerful Daksha's unjust opinions. Eventually, Sati was consumed by the fire of her anger.

Shiva was livid when he heard of his wife's death. He tore a matt of hair from his head in a rage, and using his divine powers; he molded a thousand-limbed, ferocious monster named Virabhadra. Shiva ordered his son, Virabhadra, to destroy Daksha along with his supporter. Virabhadra completed this mission with resounding success, which pleased his lord and father.

Virabhadra and Shiva's other son, Lord Karthikeya, became brothers. This is the reason natives afflicted with the negative effects of Mangala Gruha pray to Lord Karthikeya for release.

Important astrological facts about Mars - Mars stands for strength and power and signifies siblings. His hierarchical position in Vedic Astrology is that of the army commander. Temperamentally, Mangala Gruha is rash, angry, and violent. He governs the fire element, and the primary quality is Tamas.

This Kshatriya's nature is malefic. His strength is felt the most when he is in the 10th House, and his power is at the weakest when he is in the fourth house. Mars rules over Aries (Mesha Rashi) and Scorpio (Vrischika Rashi). His friends are Surya, Chandra, and Guru. Only Shukra is his enemy. The Nakshatras Guja rules include Dhanishta, Mrigashirsha, and Chitra.

Guja is sometimes spelled as Kuja too. Mars is the commander in Vedic Astrology. He represents courage, energy, younger siblings, especially brothers (and hence is known as Bhatrukaraka or protector of brothers), police and armed forces, administrators, commanders, engineering, land, real estate, and other masculine kinds of activities. The metal of Mars is copper, the gem is coral, and its color is red. He represents the south direction. It takes Mars about 45 days to travel through one Zodiac Sign.

The positive emotions and behavioral attitudes connected to Mars are energy, courage, activity, originality, and initiative. The negative attitudes related to Mars are aggression, arrogance, selfishness, headstrong, and impulsive.

Buddha or Mercury

Being closest to the Sun, Mercury is a planet with a diameter of about 4800 kilometers. This planet takes 88 days to complete one revolution around the Sun and about 59 days for one rotation around its axis. It has no natural satellite of its own. Its retrograde period is about 20 to 24 days, which takes place once in approximately four months.

Buddha in Hindu Mythology - According to Hindu mythology, Buddha is Chandra, the Moon God's son. Chandra became a powerful divine being and conquered the three worlds, which led to him becoming highly arrogant. Chandra was one of the primary disciples of Guru, or Jupiter, the guru of the Devas. He was also a favorite of Jupiter's wife, Tara.

One day, when Jupiter was away, Tara and Chandra eloped. On returning home, when Jupiter found his bride missing, he realized what had happened. He sent multiple messages to Chandra to return his wife honorably to him. Chandra paid no heed to these requests, saying that Tara came of her own accord and would leave him only when she is satiated. Jupiter now turned to another of his disciples, Indra (the king of gods), for help. Indra sent an ultimatum to Chandra to return their guru's wife.

When Chandra refused to comply with his ultimatum too, Indra waged war against the Moon God. Venus (Jupiter's enemy), along with the Asuras, took Chandra's side while Lord Shiva and many devas fought alongside Indra in this war. The war went on for so long the wise sages feared the end of the world was near. Lord Brahma then ordered Chandra to return Tara to Jupiter. This time Chandra obliged, but not before making her pregnant with his child.

Jupiter forced Tara to abort Chandra's child. But the baby who was radiant and golden survived. Seeing the beauty of the baby, both the Moon and Jupiter claimed paternity. Both demanded that Tara declare the true name of the baby's father. Lord Brahma had to interfere again and asked Tara for the baby's father's name in private. At this point, Tara said that Chandra was the father of the child who was none other than Mercury or Buddha.

Important astrological facts about Mercury - known as the prince in Vedic Astrology, Mercury is a masculine planet. He represents intelligence, speech, maternal uncles, the medical profession, trade, computers and the internet, short journeys, astrology, knowledge of Shastras, journalism, mathematics, and printing and publishing. The gem of Mercury is emerald, and his metal is bronze. His color is green, and he represents the north direction. Mercury takes about a month to travel through one Zodiac sign.

Mercury is considered the god of speech, and relationship signifies maternal uncles. In the astrological hierarchy, Mercury is the Crown Prince, while his temperament is versatile and volatile. He governs the earth element and rules two Zodiac signs, namely Gemini (Mithunah) and Virgo (Kanya Rashi).

His nature is beneficial when combined with other favorable planets. Mercury's strength is when he is in the First House, and his weak position is the seventh house. His friends are Surya and Shukra, and his enemies are Chandra and Mangala. The Nakshatras that Mercury rules over are Ashlesha, Jayeshtha, and Revati.

Positive emotions connected with Mercury include alertness, brilliance, versatility, articulateness, and dexterity. Negative elements related to Mercury are nosiness, skepticism, restlessness, indecision, and criticalness.

Shukra, or Venus

Venus is the second farthest (after Mercury) planet from the sun and is the brightest heavenly body after the sun and moon. With a diameter of about 12000 kilometers, Venus or Shukra is the closest planet to the earth. It takes about 225 days for Venus to complete one revolution around the sun and about 243 days for one rotation around its axis. Venus has no natural satellite. Its retrograde period is about 40-43 days, which happens once every 19 months.

Shukra in Hindu Mythology - Shukra was the guru of the Daityas or Asuras. He knew the secret use of Sanjivini Vidya with which it was possible to revive the dead. He used this powerful knowledge to revive dead asuras. Also, Shukra was immensely learned and an astute Brahmin. He was handsome, intelligent, and sensuous. His father was Rishi Bhrigu, and his mother was Puloma.

One day, Venus was enjoying the beauty of nature as his father, Rishi Bhrigu, was deep in meditation nearby. Venus fell hopelessly in love with Apsara Viswachi, who had come to that spot. He followed her to heaven and created a small hut for her, living happily with Viswachi for many years until the effects of his good karma ended.

When his good karmas ended, Shukra's soul fell to the moon and then to the earth, where he was born as the son of a virtuous Brahmin. He led an austere life on Mount Meru for a long time until he met Viswachi again, who was cursed to be born as a female deer. Shukra fell in love with the deer, and through their union, a human child was born.

Then, the life of the Brahmin who held Shukra's soul ended. After his death, Shukra was reborn as the prince of Madra, which he ruled for many years. Like this, Shukra's soul was reborn multiple times on earth until his final birth was that of a son of a learned seer who lived on the banks of a river.

Meanwhile, Rishi Bhrigu opened his eyes after thousands of human years had passed and saw the worn-out body of his dead son, Shukra. In anger, he was about to curse Yama, the Lord of Death, who appeared before him and reminded him that Shukra's karma resulted in his multiple births and deaths. And that, right then, he was meditating on earth on the banks of a river.

The Lord of Death revived Shukra's body, who realized the truth behind his numerous births and deaths he had to undertake to cleanse himself of all karmic effects. Venus then meditated on Lord Shiva to achieve spiritual salvation. After thousands of years of meditation, Lord Shiva appeared to Shukra, taught him the Sanjivini Vidya, and gave him the boon of being the most auspicious planet among the nine planets.

Even today, marriages are performed only when Venus is rising in the sky. After that, Shukra had many wives and was blessed with several children too.

Important astrological facts about Venus - Venus is the guru of the demons or asuras and is known as Daitya guru. He represents sex life and sex organs, kidneys, spouse (and hence is called *Kalatrakaraka)*, dance, music and the arts, gems and jewels, bars, wines, gambling dens, fashion and cosmetics, and beauty products. The metal of Venus is silver, his color is white, his gem is diamond, and he represents the southeast direction. The planet Venus takes about a month to travel one Rashi, and like the Sun, takes one year to complete one round of the Zodiac.

Venus' significance is connected to desire and potency. He represents the spousal relationship. In the astrological hierarchy, Venus or Shukra is the Royal Advisor or Minister. His nature is accommodating, easy-going, and beneficial to everyone. Venus is related to the water element, and this primary Guna is Rajas, which stands for passion and imperiousness.

Venus' strength is at its peak when he is in the Fourth House, and he is the weakest in the 10th house. The Zodiac Signs he rules over are Taurus (Vrishabha Rashi) and Libra (Tula Rashi). His friends are Mercury (Buddha) and Shani (Saturn). His enemies are Surya and Chandra. He is neutral with Jupiter (Guru) and Mars (Mangala). Venus is the ruling planet of Bharani, Purva Phalguni, and Purvashada Nakshatras.

Venus relates to harmony, refinement, devotion, responsiveness, and affection. The negative emotions connected with Venus are indifference, laziness, superficial, flirtatious, and self-indulgence.

Guru, Brihaspathi, or Jupiter

Jupiter is the biggest planet in our Solar System, with a diameter of 142 800 kilometers. It takes 11.86 years to complete one revolution around the Sun and a little less than 10 hours to complete one rotation about its axis. Jupiter has 63 natural satellites. It retrogrades for about 110 days every approximately once every year.

Guru in Hindu Mythology - Guru or Brihaspati was one of Rishi Angiras' eight sons. His mother and Rishi Angiras' wife was Shraddha. After receiving the basic knowledge from his father, he left home in search of spiritual intelligence. He meditated for thousands of years to gain insight and wisdom. His relentless penances earned him a position of guru to the gods. His primary purpose was to protect and advance the interests of the devas (or gods) and thwart the designs and intentions of demons (or Asuras).

Once Shukra, the guru of the Asuras, went to the Himalayas to meditate and seek the power to conquer and destroy the devas from Lord Shiva. Indra, the devas' king, sent his daughter, Jayanthi, to deceive Shukra with her amorous charms and learn whatever Lord Shiva would teach him. She stayed with Shukra for many years until Lord Shiva appeared and taught them everything they wanted to learn.

When it was time to return to the devas' abode, Jayanthi had a change of heart. She revealed her true identity to Shukra and requested him to accept her as his wife. He agreed to her request but said he would be with her only for 10 years, and during this period, they would live alone.

Jupiter used this period of 10 years to disguise himself as Shukra so he could live with the Asuras and remove hatred and factionalism among them. Guru disguised as Shukra endeared himself to the Asuras. When the real Shukra returned, the Asuras were confused by two identical-looking gurus. They declared Jupiter (disguised as Shukra) to be their real guru. The real Shukra got angry and cursed them they would be destroyed soon.

Soon after, Jupiter changed into true form and left the Asuras' abode and went to the heavens. The demons now realized their mistake and rushed to their real guru and begged for his forgiveness. He relented and returned to be their guru. But his curse could not be taken back, and the Asuras became very weak to threaten the devas. In this way, Jupiter served his ardent followers, the devas.

Important astrological facts about Jupiter - Brihaspathi or Guru is known as the Devaguru or the guru to the gods. He represents spirituality, wisdom, temples, priests, research and science, teachers, lawyers and judges, and knowledge of astrology and other Shastras in the Sanatana Dharma. The metal of Jupiter is gold, the gem is the yellow sapphire, and the direction he represents is northeast. Guru takes one year to travel through one zodiac sign. Known as Putrakaraka, he is the protector of and connected with children and offspring.

Jupiter is related to fortune and knowledge. He represents the relationship with children, and like Shukra, holds a ministerial or advisory position in the Vedic astrological hierarchy. Jupiter's nature is benign, gentle, and mild. He governs the element, ether. His primary Guna is Sattva representing peace and serenity. His power is at its peak when he is in the first house and the weakest when he is in the seventh house.

Jupiter rules over Dhanush and Meena Rashis. His friends are Surya, Chandra, and Mangala, while his enemies are Buddha and Shukra. He has a neutral relationship with Shani. The three Nakshatras that Jupiter rules over include Punarvasu, Vishakha, and Purva Bhadra.

The positive emotions related to Jupiter are expansion, understanding, opportunity, enthusiasm, and optimism. The negative emotions connected with Jupiter are extravagance, indulgence, bigotry, smugness, and fanaticism.

Shani, or Saturn

With a 120 660 kilometers diameter, Saturn is the second-largest planet in our Solar System after Jupiter. Jupiter's most famous aspect concerns the complex ring system surrounding it. Saturn takes 29.5 years to complete one revolution around the Sun and a little less than 11 hours to complete one rotation about its axis. Saturn has 62 natural satellites, of which Titan is the largest satellite in our Solar System. Shani goes into retrograde once a year for about 135 days.

Shani in Hindu Mythology - Shani is represented as being very tall (with long limbs), with black skin, reddish-brown eyes, and an emaciated look. He is cruel in authoritative positions, and his gaze can terrify anyone. Shani is the son of Surya and his second wife, Chaaya. His brother is Lord Yama, the god of death and righteousness.

As soon as Shani was born, he looked at his father, Surya, who immediately got afflicted with vitiligo. Next, Shani looked at Arun, Surya's charioteer, who fell and broke his thighs. When he next gazed at the seven horses of Surya's chariot, their eyes turned to stone, and they became blind.

The Sun God tried various remedies to cure everyone. Although, nothing worked. Only when Saturn turned his gaze away did Surya's skin cleared, Arun's thighs were healed, and the seven horses got back their eyesight. Shani performed many years of penance at the holy city of Benares, where Lord Shiva appeared before him and gave him the position of a planet in the Zodiac.

Shani is the god of longevity, justice, death, and time. Even the king of gods, Indra, panics when Shani is nearby because thousands of Indras have been consumed by the power of time.

Important astrological facts about Shani - Shani is a servant in the hierarchy of Vedic Astrology. He represents sorrow, hard work, old men, servants, and other lower-level workers such as those in the iron and steel industry, drainage work, and municipality. Saturn placed in the right position on the Rashi chart can bestow prestige and power on the native. But Saturn in the wrong place can cause havoc and devastation in the life of the native.

Saturn's color is blue, his metal is iron, the gem is blue sapphire, and he represents the west direction. He is the slowest moving planet taking about 2 and ½ years in each Zodiac. Therefore, he takes 30 years to complete one round of the Zodiac. He is called Udyoga karaka because he is connected to professions.

He is connected to grief and misfortune. He represents subordinates or the workers at the lower order. The temperament of Saturn is cruel, harsh, and insensitivity. His nature is malefic. He is related to the Air element, and his primary Guna is Tamas, which stands for dullness and ignorance.

His strength is at its peak when Shani is in the seventh house, and he is weakest when he is in the first house. He rules over Makar and Kumbh Rashis. His friends are Shukra and Buddha, his enemies are Surya, Chandra, and Mangala, and he has a neutral relationship with Guru. The three Nakshatras he lords over include Pushya, Anuradha, and Uttara Bhadra.

The positive keywords related to Shani are experience, humility, patience, compassion, and wisdom. The negative emotions connected with Saturn are sorrow, challenges, delay, limitation, and disappointment.

Rahu, or the Dragon's Head, or the Lunar North Node and Ketu, or the Dragon's Tail, or the Lunar South Node

According to Vedic Astrology, Rahu and Ketu stand for the two points of intersection between the Sun and Moon's paths as they move around in the Zodiac. They are called the *south and north lunar nodes*. Eclipses occur when the Sun and the Moon are at one of these two places, which gave rise to the myth of the sun being swallowed.

Rahu and Ketu in Hindu Mythology - Rahu's father was Viprachitti, and his mother was Simhika. Simhika was the sister of Prahlad, the ardent Asura devotee of Lord Vishnu. Ketu is the dismembered body while Rahu is the head. Their story is part of the story of Amrit Manthan or the Churning of the Ocean.

The devas were losing their power, thanks to Sage Durvasa's curse. The king of devas, Indra, lost his kingdom to the Asuras. They went to Lord Brahma for help, who directed them to go to Lord Vishnu. Vishnu told Indra to approach the Asuras and ask for their help in churning the ocean so they could both get *amrita*, the nectar of immortality. Indra suggested to the Asuras that both could share the nectar and become immortal. The Asuras agreed to help in the churning of the ocean.

Mount Mandara was used as a rod, and Serpent Vasuki was used as a churning rope. Lord Vishnu took the form of a gigantic tortoise to hold up Mount Mandara and prevent it from slipping into the ocean. As the churning began, the Asuras on one side and the devas on the other, many things emerged from the ocean.

The poison, halahala, was the first thing that came up. It threatened to destroy both the devas and asuras. But Lord Shiva came to their rescue. He swallowed the poison and held it at this throat for eternity. Other important elements that emerged from the churning included the celestial horse, Ucchaishravas, Kamadhenu, the wish-fulfilling cow, Airavata, the white celestial elephant, Lakshmi, the goddess of wealth and prosperity, Apsaras, the beautiful dancers, the Kausthubha gem, and much more. Finally, the god of medicine, Dhanvantri, emerged holding a pot filled with amrita. The asuras snatched it and refused to share it with the devas.

At this time, Lord Vishnu was Mohini, an irresistible enchantress whom the asuras lusted after. They handed over the pot of nectar to Mohini and agreed to allow her to distribute the amrita as per her wishes. She asked the devas and asuras to sit in a line and distributed the nectar, beginning with the devas.

Rahu realized something was amiss. He disguised himself as a deva and sat between Surya and Chandra, who recognized him immediately. Vishnu, in the form of Mohini, threw his discus and severed Rahu's head. But Rahu managed to drink one tiny drop of the nectar, making himself immortal just in time.

Therefore, although his head and body were separate, both the parts remained immortal. The head was called Rahu, and the headless body got the name Ketu. These two are continually chasing the Sun and Moon gods because they were the ones who sneaked to Mohini about his presence. When they catch him, they swallow the sun and moon, causing solar and lunar eclipses. But, as Rahu and Ketu cannot hold him for long, the sun and moon come out intact because they have also had their share of the nectar of immortality.

Important astrological facts about Rahu - This shadow planet represents foreign countries, foreigners, international travel, smoke, engineering and technical industries and trade, drinking, gambling, grandparents. He also represents the underworld and the dark, shadow life in a society. Rahu's color is black, he represents a mixed metal, and his gem is Gomedh or hessonite garnet. Rahu takes about 1 and ½ years to travel a Zodiac sign, and therefore, takes 18 years to complete one round of the Zodiac.

Rahu represents maternal grandparents and is known for spiritual knowledge. He represents the air element. Rahu lords over Ardra, Swati, and Shatabhisha Nakshatras. Rahu's positive keywords are independence, originality, inspiration, insight, and imagination and negative keywords are deception, confusion, addiction, illusion, and neurosis.

Important Astrological Facts About Ketu - Representing grandparents, spiritual inclinations, technical and electronics trades, superstitions, Ketu, like Rahu, takes about 1 and ½ years to complete one Zodiac. Ketu represents paternal grandparents and stands for moksha or ultimate liberation. The temperaments of both Rahu and Ketu are unpredictable and erratic. Ketu represents the fire element. The primary quality of Rahu and Ketu is Tamas. Their natures of both planets are malefic.

Ketu rules over Ashwini, Magha, and Moola Nakshatra. Rahu and Ketu's friends are Shukra, Mangala, and Shani, their enemies are Surya and Chandra, and they have a neutral relationship with Guru and Buddha. Ketu's positive keywords are self-sacrifice, idealism, spirituality, compassion, and intuition, and negative keywords are eccentricity, fanaticism, amorality, violence, and impulsiveness.

Each of the nine planets has different effects, good and bad, on the native's life depending on their placements in the various Rashis. Interestingly, the effects on a person's life could be diagrammatically opposite to that of another individual. Seven out of the nine (Rahu and Ketu are left out) planets also rule the seven days of the week as under:

- Surya rules Sunday.
- Chandra rules Monday.
- Mangala rules Tuesday.
- Buddha rules Wednesday.
- Guru rules Thursday.

- Shukra rules Friday.
- Shani rules Saturday.

Now that you have a good idea about the nine planets and their significance, it is time to see how they influence our daily lives.

Chapter 3: Planetary Influences on Daily Life

Understanding planetary influences on our daily life requires us to know more about the relationships shared by the nine planets, their positions on the Zodiac, and the direct and special aspects of each planet. Let us know more about these and other elements in Vedic Astrology.

Five-Fold Relationship

Called *Panchada Maitri* in Sanskrit, planetary relationships are complex. It is important to know that the power of a planet depends on his own position and the relative position with other planets. Planets are powerful if they are in any one of these positions:

- In the house of the sign(s) of their exaltation.
- In their own house.
- In the house of their friends.

Planets are weak when, in one of these positions:

- In the house of their enemies.
- In the house of the sign(s) of their debilitation.

The strength of the planets is neutral in the house of neutral signs.

When two planets have a relationship-based influence over each other, then the effects on the concerned natives depend on the quality of these interplanetary relations. The planets have different relationships and friends, including a great (or fast) friend (ati mitra), a good friend (mitra), neutral (sama), bitter enemies (ati shatru), and enemies or inimical (shatru). This concept is called *Panchada Maitri*, which is of four types of relationships, including:

Parivartana or Exchange Relationship - This two-way exchange is the most powerful of all the four types. It is based on mutual sign ownership. This happens when two planets are in two houses owned by each other.

Aspect or Drishti Relationship - This is a one-way exchange wherein one planet is in the house owned by another planet. Also, the house is aspected significantly. If the aspect is almost total, then this relationship is also very powerful.

Posited in the Same Sign - When two planets are posited together in the same sign, then too, the exchange is powerful.

Mutual Aspect - This happens when two planets mutually aspect each other. If this happens at near-total levels, then too, the exchange can be powerful.

The interplanetary relationships of each planet are also determined by their Tatkalik (temporal) and Naisargik (natural or permanent) friendships. Permanent friendships and relationships depend on the planets' natural status, whereas temporal relationships depend on the position of the planets in individual horoscopes.

The third relationship is the neutral type (or Sama), wherein the planets are neither friends nor enemies but are neutral towards each other. Both enjoy equal status. The relation is always seen from the perspective of the planet under consideration. For example, suppose you want to see the link of Surya with other planets. There, its tie is judged from Surya's viewpoint and is independent of the other planet's attitudes toward Surya.

Chart analysis is rarely done using Naisargika relationships. It is only used to compute Panchadha Maitree. The temporal links are the ones used for chart analysis. So, if Chandra is not hostile towards any planet in its Naisargika relationships, then it only means that in the Panchada Maitri Scheme, he will never be a sworn enemy of other planets. Although, if there is hostility from Chandra's perspective in the Tatkalika relationships, then it can be hostile to another planet in the Panchada Maitri Scheme.

Naisargika friendship works like this. Satyacharya's rule governs Naisargika relationships. From the Mooltrikona sign of any graha, the lords of the 2nd, 4th, 5th, 8th, 9th, 12th, and the lord of the exaltation sign are his friends. The lords of the other houses, namely the 3rd, 6th, 7th, 10th, and 11th, are hostile towards this planet. But the lord of the planet's exaltation sign will also be a friend, even if he is in one of the inimical houses. The lords who own both are neutral. If a planet becomes a friend and enemy because of owning two houses, then it is considered a neutral planet.

Naisargika friendships are permanent and are not influenced by the position of the planets in the elliptical. The planets are friendly or hostile due to their inherent characteristics. The rays of the planet will be intensified by the rays of mitra planets and counteracted or weakened by enemy or shatru planets.

Tatkalik relationships work like this. The planets in the second, third, fourth, eleventh, or twelfth houses from each planet become temporary mitra or friends, and the planets in the other houses are temporarily inimical.

Panchada Maitri is arrived at by combining Naisargika and Tatkalika friends:

- If two planets are friendly in both Naisargika and Tatkalika perspectives, then they are extremely friendly in the native's horoscope; permanent friend + temporary friend = best friend.

- If they are friendly through one view and have a neutral relationship through the other, then the result is friendly; permanent friend + temporary enemy = neutral.

- If enmity combines with affinity, then the result is equality; permanent enemy + temporary friend = neutral

- Enmity combining with neutral results in enmity.

- If there is enmity from both accounts, then the result is extreme enmity; permanent enemy + temporary enemy = bitter enemy.

The Mooltrikona positions of the seven planets are:

- Surya in Simha Rashi up to 20-degrees.
- Chandra in Vrishabha Rashi up to 27-degrees.
- Mangala in Mesha Rashi up to 12-degrees.
- Buddha in Kanya Rashi up to 20-degrees.
- Guru in Dhanush Rashi up to 10-degrees.
- Shukra in Tula Rashi up to 15-degrees.
- Shani in Kumbha Rashi up to 20-degrees.

Using these rules, the friendship-enmity relationships of Naisargika friendship for each of the seven planets is:

Surya - Surya represents good fortune, soul, career, father-figure, and authority. The aspects of the Sun are not malefic in nature. However, he can cause feelings of cruelty, egotistical acts, and selfishness.

The Mooltrikona is Simha Rashi (Leo). The 4th, 2nd, 12th, 5th, 9th, and 8th houses hold Mangala, Buddha, Chandra, Guru, Mangala, and Guru, respectively. Surya's sign of exaltation is Mangala. Therefore, Mangala, Buddha, Chandra, and Guru are his friends.

The lords of the 3rd, 6th, 7th, 10th, and 11th in relation to Surya are Shukra, Shani, Shani, Shukra, and Buddha. Shani and Shukra are Surya's enemies. Buddha holds a house of a friend and that of an enemy for Surya. Buddha has a neutral relationship with Surya.

Chandra - Chandra or the Moon desires family, mind, and the mind's obsessions and home. The Mooltrikona of Chandra in Vrishabha Rashi (Taurus). The 4th, 2nd, 12th, 5th, 9th, and 8th houses hold Surya, Buddha, Mangala, Buddha, Shani, Guru, who are Chandra's friends. Chandra's exaltation sign is Shukra, who is also Chandra's friend, regardless of the house he occupies.

The lords of the 3rd, 6th, 7th, 10th, and 11th, in relation to Chandra's Mooltrikona, are Chandra, Shukra, Mangala, Shani, and Guru, respectively. Shukra has an inimical position with respect to Chandra and his sign of exaltation. Shukra's relationship with Chandra is neutral. Similarly, Mangala, Shani, and Guru will have a neutral exchange with Chandra because they share a friendly and an inimical relationship.

Buddha - Buddha or Mercury represents speech, intellect, learning and understanding, communication, and profession. The Mooltrikona of Buddha is Kanya Rashi (Virgo). The lords of the 4th, 2nd, 12th, 5th, 9th, and 8th houses in accord to Buddha's position are Guru, Shukra, Surya, Shani, Shukra, and Mangala, resulting in a friendly relationship with Buddha (Mercury). The sign of exaltation is Mercury himself.

The lords of the 3rd, 6th, 7th, 10th, and 11th houses are Mangala, Shani, Guru, Buddha, and Chandra. Using the Panchada Maitri rules, Mangala and Shani have a neutral relationship with Buddha because they are lords of friendly and an inimical house in accord to Buddha's Mooltrikona position.

Shukra - Shukra or Venus represents love, sensuality, peace, sex, materialistic comforts, and love-based relationships. The Mooltrikona of Shukra is Tula Rashi (Libra). The lords of the 4th, 2nd, 12th, 5th, 9th, and 8th houses in relationship to Shukra are Shani, Mangala, Buddha, Shani, Buddha, and Shukra, respectively, giving them a friendly relationship. The sign of exaltation of Shukra is Guru.

The lords of the 3rd, 6th, 7th, 10th, and 11th houses are Guru, Guru, Mangala, Chandra, and Surya, subsequently, giving them an inimical relationship with Shukra. Guru and Mangala will have a neutral link with Shukra as each occupies a friendly and an inimical house.

Mangala - Mangala or Mars desires and represents conflicts, ambition, power, and property. The Mooltrikona of Mangala (Mars) is Mesha Rashi (Aries). The lords of the 4th, 2nd, 12th, 5th, 9th, and 8th houses in relationship to Mars are Chandra, Shukra, Guru, Surya, Guru, and Mangala, respectively, giving them a friendly link with Mars. The sign of exaltation of Mangala is Shani.

The lords of the 3rd, 6th, 7th, 10th, and 11th houses regarding Mars' Mooltrikona position are Buddha, Buddha, Shukra, Shani, and Shani, then giving them a relationship of enmity. Shukra and Shani will have a neutral relationship with Mangala because they occupy a friendly and an inimical position.

Guru - Guru represents knowledge, spirituality, good fortune, values, and religion. The Mooltrikona of Guru (Jupiter) is Dhanush Rashi (Sagittarius). The lords of the 4th, 2nd, 12th, 5th, 9th, and 8th houses in relationship to Guru's Mooltrikona position are Guru, Shani, Mangala, Mangala, Surya, and Chandra, resulting in a friendly relationship. Guru's sign of exaltation is Chandra.

The lords of the 3rd, 6th, 7th, 10th, and 11th houses regarding Guru are Shani, Shukra, Buddha, Buddha, and Shukra, resulting in an inimical relationship. Shani has a neutral relationship with Guru.

Shani - Shani represents suffering, hard work, poverty, illness, and finality. The Mooltrikona of Shani (Saturn) is Kumbh Rashi (Aquarius). he lords of the 4th, 2nd, 12th, 5th, 9th, and 8th houses in relationship to Shani are Shukra, Guru, Shani, Buddha, and Shukra, respectively, giving them a friendly relation. The sign of exaltation of Shani is Shukra.

The lords of the 3rd, 6th, 7th, 10th, and 11th houses regarding Shani are Mangala, Chandra, Surya, Mangala, and Guru, giving them a relationship of enmity with Shani. Guru shares a neutral relationship with Shani because he occupies a friendly and an inimical position.

Natural Friends and Enemies of Rahu and Ketu

Rahu stands for manipulation, enjoyment, and ambition. He can cause cheating, shocks, and losses for natives. Rahu's Mooltrikona is Mithuna Rashi (Gemini). So, his friends should be the lords of Cancer, Virgo, Libra, Capricorn, Aquarius, and Taurus. His enemies would be the lords of Leo, Scorpio, Sagittarius, Pisces, and Aries.

Rahu's exaltation sign is Taurus, which is the 12th house from his Mooltrikona, already a friendly position. According to the Panchada Maitri rules, Chandra, Shukra, and Rahu are natural friends of Rahu, whereas Surya, Mangala, and Guru are his natural enemies. Buddha is neutral.

Ketu has no aspects because he represents no desires. Ketu's Mooltrikona is Dhanush Rashi (Sagittarius). So, Ketu's friendly signs are Capricorn, Pisces, Aries, Leo, Cancer, and Scorpio. His enemy signs are Aquarius, Taurus, Gemini, Virgo, and Libra. Ketu's exaltation sign is Scorpio, which is already in a friendly relationship occupying the 12th house.

Ketu's friends are Surya, Chandra, and Mangala, while his natural enemies are Shukra and Buddha. Shani and Guru have a neutral relationship with Ketu.

The following list summarizes the friends, enemies, and neutral relationships of the nine planets:

Surya - Surya's (or the Sun) friends are Moon (Chandra), Mars (Mangala), and Jupiter (Guru). His enemies are Shukra (Venus), Shani (Saturn), and Rahu. Neutral planets are Buddha and Ketu.

Chandra - Chandra's (or the Moon) friends are Surya and Shukra. His enemies are none, and he has a neutral relationship with Mangala, Guru, Shukra, Shani, Rahu, and Ketu.

Buddha - Buddha's (or Mercury) friends are Surya and Shukra. His enemies are Chandra and Ketu. He has neutral relationships with Mangala, Guru, Shani, and Rahu.

Shukra - Shukra (or Venus) friends are Buddha, Shani, and Rahu. His enemies are Surya and Chandra. He has a neutral relationship with Mangala, Guru, and Ketu.

Mangala - Mangala's (Mars) friends are Surya, Chandra, and Guru. His enemy is Buddha. And he is neutral with Shukra, Shani, Rahu, and Ketu.

Guru - Guru's (or Jupiter) friends are Surya, Chandra, and Mangala. His enemies are Buddha, Shukra, and Rahu. Guru has a neutral relationship with Shani and Ketu.

Shani - Shani's (or Saturn) friends are Buddha, Shukra, and Rahu. His enemies are Surya, Chandra, Mangala, and Rahu. He has a neutral relationship with Buddha and Guru.

Rahu - Rahu's friends are Shukra and Shani. His enemies are Surya, Chandra, and Mangala. He has a neutral relationship with Buddha, Guru, and Ketu.

Ketu - Ketu's friends are Surya and Mangala. His enemies are Shukra and Shani. He has a neutral relationship with Buddha, Guru, Chandra, and Rahu.

Reciprocal and Non-Reciprocal Friendships, Enmity, and Relationships

Surya is friendly with Mangala, Guru, and Chandra. These three planets, in turn, reciprocate the friendship towards Surya. Surya's enemies are Shani and Shukra, and they, in turn, are Surya's enemies. These relationships are termed as reciprocal.

Now, let us take another example. Surya is tolerant or neutral towards Buddha. Interestingly, Buddha likes Surya and considers him to be a friend. This kind of relationship is termed as non-reciprocal. The non-reciprocal types of relationships are interesting ones and give us a lot of insight and information into life.

Non-reciprocal friendships are ambiguously explained in the various texts of Vedic Astrology. But the most important component to support friendships and enmity of a planet with other planets is the planet itself, the one posited in the Mooltrikona, which is being considered. Parashara's text clearly states that the feelings of that planet towards other planets should be the determining factor of its relationships with other planets.

Logically too, this interpretation makes a lot of sense. Let us look at an example of the non-reciprocal relationship between Surya and Buddha to understand this interpretation. Now, Surya or the Sun represents authority and the soul or the consciousness. Buddha represents free speech and intellect. There is a complex but inevitable relationship between authority, consciousness, free speech, and intellect.

Mercury, the representative of free speech and intellect, likes Surya because both representative elements, namely intellect and free speech, need the support and help of authority/government and the illumination of the consciousness or the soul. So, Buddha or Mercury likes Surya.

Now, let us look at Surya and Buddha's relationship from Surya's (the representative of authority) perspective. The government or people in authority are not fond of those using free speech or free thinkers. Freethinkers and supporters of free speech are tolerated but not hated. So, Surya is neutral towards, in other words, he "tolerates" Buddha. This interpretation works for nearly all non-reciprocal relationships. Here are a few more examples which are useful tools to remember relationships between planets.

Mercury's non-reciprocal relationships - Next, let us look at Buddha in a little more detail. Mercury likes Venus (Shukra), who reciprocates this friendship happily, which is a reciprocal relationship. Mercury tolerates Mars (Mangala). But Mangala hates Buddha. Again, it is easy to understand logically. Mars represents the military who hate free thinkers, represented by Mercury. Freethinkers, on the other hand, put up or tolerate the military and the police because free thinkers not only understand the perspectives of the police and military, but they also need them for protection and security.

Another non-reciprocal relationship of Mercury is with Saturn. Mercury is neutral (or tolerates) Shani, whereas Shani likes Mercury. Shani is antagonistic towards authority, which can turn off Mercury. Although Mercury is lighthearted, he can tolerate Shani but cannot be on friendly terms.

Mercury and Jupiter (Guru) also share a non-reciprocal relationship. While Jupiter hates Mercury, Mercury is tolerant towards Jupiter. Jupiter stands for religion and dogma. Freethinkers and free speech supporters are continuously finding ways to embarrass religious dogmas even if they are open to (or neutral towards) religion. At this juncture, it might make sense to recall Shukra's mythology (born of Chandra and Tara, wife of Guru), who is the bastard son of Jupiter. So, while Mercury embarrasses his stepfather, Jupiter hates his bastard son.

Venus' non-reciprocal relationships - Venus is a friend of Saturn and Mercury, and both these planets reciprocate the relationship. In Vedic Astrology, the friendship between Venus (Shukra) and Saturn (Shani) is of legendary quality and is believed to be one of the strongest relationships, comparable to the relationship between Mars (Mangala) and Sun (Surya).

Venus' arch enemies are the Sun and Moon, and it is easy to understand this, considering that Venus represents creativity and the arts, both of which are usually anti-authoritarian. The Sun also dislikes Venus. But the Moon tolerates Venus' hatred.

Venus and Mars are neutral towards each other, representing the natural male-female dynamics of the universe. After all, men and women cannot live without each other, and yet find it difficult to live happily with each other, and end up tolerating one another.

Venus has a neutral relationship with Jupiter, although Jupiter does not like Venus. Again, this neutrality versus dislike non-reciprocal relationship is easy to understand. Venus stands for love, peace, and sensuality and can easily see value in religion and philosophy represented by Jupiter. While numerous forms of art and artists have been supported by religion, a lot more art-related works and people have been censored by religion.

While most artists tolerate religion, religion dislikes nearly all artists and artworks not conformed to or aligned with its beliefs and dogmas. Religion uses censorship to demonstrate its dislike for art.

Mars' Non-Reciprocal Relationships - Mars and Jupiter have a reciprocal friendly relationship. Mars representing energy and passion, knows he needs guidance represented by Jupiter. And Mars represents the enforcement agencies like the police and military, and Jupiter represents the morality-based order of enforcement, resulting in mutual, reciprocal friendship.

Mars and Saturn share a non-reciprocal relationship. Shani, representing anti-authority, hates the commanding and enforcement tendency of Mars. But Mars appreciates the practicality and tenacity of Saturn or Shani, and tolerates him.

Jupiter's Non-Reciprocal Relationship - Jupiter and Saturn tolerate each other because religion and morality (Jupiter) are inextricably intertwined with finality, represented by Saturn. Therefore, both tolerate each other even if they are totally opposite of each other.

Interestingly, no one really dislikes Jupiter, including the planets whom he ill-treats (Venus and Mercury). This likable aspect of Jupiter is based on all positive elements, including good deeds. He is a very sensitive lord and deals sensitively with others, even when doing something bad. Hence, no planet really dislikes Jupiter.

Chapter 4: House Systems and Characteristics of Bhava

Understanding the systems of houses in Vedic Astrology is the start of the basics of this fascinating subject. The Zodiac elliptical is 360-degrees, which is divided into 12 equal divisions of 30 degrees each. Each division is called a *Zodiac sign* or *house*. This 12-house system starts from Aries and finishes at Pisces.

Each of the 12 signs has one ruler (a planet), and planets rule two signs (dual ownership). An important element about dual ownership is that when a planet rules over two signs, then one of them is more important than the other. This concept is relative and is regardless of the planet and the signs it rules over. The more important sign becomes the Mooltrikona sign for that planet.

In Vedic Astrology, a planet is a heavenly body being considered in the Zodiac elliptic. The word "planet" should not be confused with its astronomical meaning. Planets need not be the same as defined by Physics and Astronomy. For example, Sun and Moon are taken as planets, even if Physics calls Sun a star and Moon a natural satellite.

To reiterate an earlier lesson, the nine primary planets of Vedic Astrology are Sun (Surya), Moon (Chandra), Mars (Mangala), Jupiter (Guru), Saturn (Shani), Mercury (Buddha), Venus (Shukra), and Rahu and Ketu. These last two are called *Shadow Planets*. Rahu and Ketu are not physical entities. They are imaginary points on the Zodiacal elliptic, where the axis of the Sun and Moon overlap, relative to earth. It is important to know that Rahu and Ketu are mathematical calculations and not physical entities like the other seven heavenly bodies collectively known as planets. The effects of Rahu and Ketu are so powerful on horoscopes that the ancient seers thought it important to give them planet status. They are always at 180-degrees from each other.

Rahu and Ketu do not rule over any signs considering they are not physical entities. But they are co-rulers of certain signs. Also, these two astrological elements are called shadow planets because they mirror the effects of the planets they are close to or the signs they occupy temporarily.

The 12 Houses or Bhavas

The 12 houses and their ruling planets are:

    1. Aries (Mesha Rashi) -ruled by Mars (Mangala); the Mool Trikona (MK) sign for Mars in Aries

    2. Taurus (Vrishabha Rashi) - ruled by Venus (Shukra)

    3. Gemini (Mithuna Rashi) - ruled by Mercury (Buddha)

    4. Cancer (Karkata Rashi) - ruled by Moon (Chandra)

    5. Leo (Simha Rashi) - ruled by Sun (Surya)

    6. Virgo (Kanya Rashi) - ruled by Buddha and Rahu - MK sign of Buddha

    7. Libra (Tula Rashi - ruled by Shukra (MK sign)

    8. Scorpio (Vrishchika Rashi) - ruled by Mars (Mangala) and Ketu

9. Sagittarius (Dhanush Rashi) - ruled by Jupiter (Guru) - MK sign

10. Capricorn (Makar Rashi) -ruled by Saturn

11. Aquarius (Kumbh Rashi) - ruled by Saturn (MK sign) and Rahu (co-ruler)

12. Pisces (Meena Rashi) - ruled by Jupiter

The term "Bhava" in Sanskrit means state or condition. In Jyotishya, Bhava is used to denote a fixed division in the Zodiac. It corresponds to the term 'house' used in Western Astrology. A natal or birth chart in Vedic Astrology is called *bhavachakra*, where chakra means "wheel" or "circle".

All charts have the same twelve bhavas or houses measuring 30 degrees each. The difference between individual charts is which house is taken as the first house, second house, and so forth until the 12 house. The Lagna or the Ascendant Sign determines the first house. The Lagna is the sign rising in the east at the time of the native's birth. The Lagna house is the first house for that person, and the others follow counter-clockwise, in the same sequence as the Zodiac elliptic.

The twelve houses rule over numerous aspects of an individual's life. Elements that each house rules over are given below. But it is important to remember that this list is not exhaustive.

The First House - Or the Lagna bhava, primarily represents the native's personality. It controls or rules over these aspects of a native's life, personality, behavior, physical appearances, etc.:

- The personality of the individual
- The head and the hair on the head
- Skull, skin, brain
- General health status including immunity and vitality
- Overall success, happiness, and wellbeing
- General physical characteristics of the native

- General mental characteristics
- Place of birth
- Thoughts and the working of the mind
- Power and status in society and family
- Starting of events and happenings

The Second House - Mainly stands for wealth and is called the *house of Dhana bhava* (wealth in Sanskrit). It represents and governs these aspects of the concerned native:

- It is the primary house of wealth, including assets like savings, property, retirement accounts, etc.
- Material possessions like clothes, jewelry, and household articles.
- Family of the native
- Face, mouth, and the tongue area and speech
- Left eye for the female and right eye for the male native along with general eyesight
- It is the place of death or the house with the potential to kill the native
- Basic education (until 3rd grade)

The Third House - Called *Parakrama* (courage) or *bhratru* (brothers), reflects the valor and courage of the native. It represents and governs these aspects of an individual's life:

- Siblings of the native, especially the younger siblings
- Neighbors and other people around the native
- Courage and valor of the person
- Throat and neck area including communication and speech
- Ears and hearing

- Communication aspects such as journalism, media, IT, internet, phones, computers, writing books and articles, and handwriting
- Short distance travel and short-term goals including hobbies
- Activities connected with the hands and arms
- Enthusiasm for work
- Libido and sexual prowess

The Fourth House - Called "*Suhdra*" of "*sukha*", reflects the mother relationship. rules over these aspects of a person's life:

- Mother
- Motherland
- Vehicles
- Fixed property such as land, houses, and other forms of real estate, including agricultural land
- Emotions and happiness
- Luxuries and comfort (or the lack of it)
- Place of residence
- Chest, lungs, heart, the upper part of the spine,
- Private life and feelings
- Peace of mind
- High school level education, up to Grade 12

The Fifth House - Demonstrates children of the native. It governs these elements in an individual's life:

- Creativity
- Children, an element of our creation,
- Imagination
- Romance and love-based emotions

- Memory and fluid intelligence
- Speculation including playing on the stock markets and gambling
- Competition
- Good karma of the past lives
- House of wealth
- Diplomacy
- Royal or powerful positions and fame
- College or higher education
- Stomach, the lower part of the heart, liver, kidneys, spleen, and lower back

The Sixth House - Ripu/Roga, which translates to *disease* in Sanskrit, showcases enmity and diseases of the native. rules over these aspects of our life:

- Anything that opposes us, including our rivals and enemies and people who compete with us
- Short term sickness, diseases, surgeries, injuries,
- Debt, litigation, and courts
- Breaking of relationships
- The day-to-day grind of work
- Agony and physical pain
- Service and servants
- Theft and thieves
- Animals
- Fire
- Hygiene and medicine
- Critical thoughts about ourselves and about others

- Pancreas, small intestine, lower back, kidneys, urinary bladder
- Pregnancy, only for female natives

The Seventh House - Kama reflects the sexual energy of the native. It determines these aspects of our lives:

- Relationships including how we interact with and relate to people
- Legal contracts and business contracts
- Partnerships including marriage, spouse, and married life
- Foreign places
- Foreign residence or home far from birth town
- External sexual organs, sexual habits, and sexuality
- Large intestine and anal area
- "Maraka" place or the place with the potential to end the life of the native concerned

The Eight House - *Mrityu* (or death) governs these aspects:

- Transformations
- Obstacles and turnarounds in life
- Sudden events like tragic and serious accidents and injuries
- Deep emotions and turmoil,
- Death and death like events
- Degenerate and addictive habits like alcoholism, smoking, taking drugs, etc.
- Hidden things including interest in the occult and metaphysics
- Deep research or deep-dive analysis of any area seeking to understand intriguing things

• Regenerate and spiritual habits including detachment from materialism, success

• Loans or unearned money like legacies and inheritances

• Change of lifestyle, home, job, or other activity

• Mental anguish and despair, including hopelessness

• Internal sexual organs, anal area, testes, only for males

• Chronic and incurable diseases including terminal sickness

The Ninth House - Bhagya, is the house of luck and fortune. It determines these factors of our life:

• Father, guru, boss or employer

• Destiny and luck

• Higher education, research

• Temples

• Crystallized intelligence relating to one's beliefs, religion, spirituality, meditation, etc.

• Long distance and foreign travel

• Good deeds of previous lives

• Divine blessings help

• House of wealth

• Abstract thinking

• Crossing intellectual boundaries into new cultures, beliefs, and religion

• Foreign residence

• Publishing

• Import-export

• Hips, thighs, and tailbone area

The Tenth House - Karma rules over these factors of our life:

- Career and job
- Status in public life
- External manifestation of our work
- Fame, popularity, prestige, and honor
- Rise in life
- Karma (our actions)
- Energy levels and image at the workplace
- Recognition from Government
- Powerful positions like politicians, CEOs, directors of institutes
- Management-related positions
- Knees and middle parts of the legs

The 11th House - Aya, lords over these aspects of our life:

- Gains and income
- Rewards from workplace and job including promotions
- Wealth house
- Long term desires, goals, and their fulfillment
- Elder siblings
- Ears and hearing
- Social circle, friends, and social interaction
- Recovery from diseases and illnesses
- Ankles and lower feet area
- Prize and/or recognition from authorities, including the government

The 12th House - Vyaya, determines these aspects of a native's life:
- Loss and expenses
- Letting go
- Isolation, imprisonment
- Loss of movement including being hospitalized
- Loss of freedom like being imprisonment
- Deep emotions such as grief and sadness
- Hidden life including sleep, sexual activity, hidden weaknesses, strengths, enemies
- Foreign residence and far-off isolated places
- Dreams, intuition, psychic powers
- Meditation and spirituality
- Lack of materialism
- Moksha
- Long-distance travel and settlement
- Feet, left eye for males, right eye for females
- Undiagnosable diseases
- Sleep-related problems like insomnia, somnambulism, etc.

Interesting Points about the Various Houses

The third and eighth houses or bhavas represent "Jeeva Shakti" or life force, and the 12th house deals with death, ending, or loss. Therefore, the 12th house to any bhava represents the loss or end of that bhava.

The 2nd and 7th houses are 12th houses from 3rd and 8th respectively, making them "Maraka" or killer houses. In the same way, the ninth house represents destiny and good fortune. The 12th from the 9th house is the 8th bhava, which is bad fortune and destruction.

Generally, houses 1, 5, and 9 are considered to give good things, including wealth, good health, good fortune, wisdom, education, etc. although there are other caveats to be considered for an accurate understanding of a person's birth chart. These three bhavas or houses are collectively called the "trikona" or triangle or the trine. Guru and Chandra are good when they are in the trine.

Houses 1, 4, 7, and 10 are called *Kendra* or the *Center* because they rule over most of our day-to-day life elements. These four houses are very important, and planets occupying these houses significantly influence the life of a native. The tenth house is the strongest and can overcome even the ascendant.

Houses 6, 8, and 12 are called bad houses or "dusthanas" as they stand for elements and things that oppose our happiness and bring grief, pain, losses, and agony.

A fourth category of bhavas is called *Upachaya*, remedial, or growth houses. In these houses, including the 3rd, 6th, 10th, and 11th, the malefic planets have a tendency to improve. This category is called "*increasing houses*," which means planets tend to give more over time. Shani and Mangala do well here and empower the natives with energy and strength to overcome obstacles. Malefic planets do well in the 11th house.

Apachaya or the houses of decrease include 1st, 2nd, 4th, 7th, and 8th bhavas, where the planets lose their strength. Malefics do not do well in these houses.

Another category called *succedent* or *fixed* includes the 2nd, 5th, 8th, and 11th bhavas. They reflect the accumulation and maintenance of our resources.

The cadent category includes the 3rd, 6th, 9th, and 12th houses. They give flexibility, intelligence, and adaptability. But they can get unstable and uncertain, leading to mental and nervous issues.

Further, the 12 houses or bhavas are divided into four categories based on the four important goals of human life as follows:

1. **Dharma** - 1st, 5th, and 9th houses stand for *dharma*, which reflects our need to find the path and purpose of our lives.

2. **Artha** - the 2nd, 6th, and 10th houses represent the *artha* or wealth creation. These three bhavas reflect the human need to acquire the necessary materialistic abilities and resources to achieve our purpose.

3. **Kama** - the 3rd, 7th, and 11th houses stand for pleasure and enjoyment, a basic need of human life.

4. **Moksha** - the 4th, 8th, and 12th houses represent our desire for enlightenment and freedom from the struggle of the limitless cycles of birth and death.

Understanding Bhavatah Bhava

Bhavatah bhava means the future bhava from a particular house. Bhavat translates to "future." Bhavatah Bhava applies to the house that is the same number as the house counted from the Lagna bhava. Bhavatah Bhava is like a house or bhava being born again in the future. Bhavatah bhava is an important technique used in Vedic

Astrology to make accurate predictions. Let us look at examples to better understand the concept of Bhavatah Bhava:

- The 3rd bhava or house because it is the 2nd house of the 2nd house. Counted in the same way (considering houses are counted counterclockwise in a circular path), the 3rd house is also the bhavatah bhava of the 8th house (because it is the 8th from the 8th house). In the same way, the following bhavatah bhavas can be arrived at:

- The 11th house is the bhavatah bhava for the 12th (12th from 12th) and the 6th (6th from the 6th house).

- The 5th house is the bhavatah bhava for the 3rd house and the 9th house.

- The 9th house is the bhavatah bhava for the 11th and the 5th houses.

- The 7th house is the bhavatah bhava for 4th and the 10th houses.

- The 1st house is the bhavatah bhava for the 7th house.

In this concept, the bhavatah bhava concept reflects sharing similar indications. For example, the 5th house stands for intellect and reflects the wisdom and deep learning. The 9th house, which is the bhavatah bhava for the 5th house, also supports these attributes as it stands for higher education or university education.

Similarly, the 5th bhava supports and aligns with the indicators of the 3rd house. To recall, the 3rd house reflects initiation into meditation and spiritual practices. The 5th house supports this by pursuing deep knowledge, wisdom, mantra chanting, etc. The reverse is also true. The 5th house reflects an appreciation for entertainment, and the 3rd house supports this aspect because it reflects music and drama.

With this basic understanding of house systems and bhavas, we can now move on to Siddhant Shastra in the next chapter.

Chapter 5: Siddhant Shastra: Mathematical and Astronomical Principles

We will focus on the basic astronomical and mathematical background of Vedic Astrology. These aspects of Vedic Astrology are described in Siddhant Shastra, which deals primarily with the calculations of lunar and solar months, the speed and distance of planets and constellations, and axes' calculations of the various planets.

The Surya Siddhanta, translated to "The Treatise of the Sun," is a Sanskrit text in Indian Astronomy. With 14 chapters, this 8th-century text describes detailed rules and formulas to calculate the planets' motions relative to the 12 asterisms. It also describes how to calculate the orbits of heavenly bodies.

The Surya Siddhanta asserts that the earth is spherical and that it orbits the sun. It does not mention Uranus and other faraway planets. It is easy to understand this, considering there were no telescopes and viewing these far-off planets was impossible through the naked eye.

Understanding Ayanamsa

Ayan means precession or movement or motion, and Amsha means a "portion" or "part". Ayanamsa translates to a part or portion of the movement (relating to heavenly bodies). Ayanamsa refers to the amount of precession. It stands for the angular difference between the vernal equinox and sidereal Zodiac.

Ayanamsa is the reason there could be differences in calculating Dasas among the various astrologers. Ayanamsa's idea plays an important role in determining divisional charts, determining planetary positions, Dasas, transits, and more. Ayanamsa usage can bring about significant changes in Dasa balances and in high-precision Varga Charts such as Shastiamsa.

We must understand the concept of the preceding equinoxes to improve our understanding of the meaning and effects of Ayanamsa. What are equinoxes? When the celestial equator intersects the ecliptic (or the path of the planets), two points of intersection are created, namely the Spring Equinox and the Fall Equinox.

Spring Equinox falls on March 21st, while the Fall Equinox is on September 21st every year. The Rashis or planets passing through these two equinoxes are continually changing. The Rashis continuously precede these equinoxes, taking 25800 years for all the Rashis to pass through these two equinoxes once. The Rashis get preceded, which is called the *preceding of the equinox*.

Ayanamsa is the difference in the angular distance created each time there is a precession in the equinox. According to Siddhanta Shastra, the precession happens at the rate of one degree every 72 years, which translates to about 50 seconds every year. Ayanamsa can be defined as the difference between tropical (Western) and sidereal (Vedic Astrology) Zodiac. The seemingly small difference is left out for calculations in Western Astrology, whereas it is included in Sidereal or Vedic Astrology leading to more specific calculations, and therefore, increasingly accurate predictions in the latter.

In 285 A.D., the positions of the planets in both the Sidereal and Tropical systems were in sync, which means in that year, there was no Ayanamsa, and there was no precession in that year. In 285 A.D., the planetary positions were the same in both the western and Vedic astrological systems.

But, as precessions started, the differences between the two systems started, and continues to do so, and will continue at the rate of approximately one degree every 72 years. So, in 285 A.D., the ayanamsa was 0, and in 2010, the value was approximately 24 degrees, which means to say, one must subtract the planet position in the tropical version by 24 degrees to arrive at the sidereal length.

The vernal equinox is the position used to measure planetary longitudes and is known as the planet's sayana position. Sayana means "along with the component of differences in degrees". The Nirayana longitude position is obtained after applying the ayanamsa correction to the value of the sayana position. Nirayana means "without the difference in degrees." Western Astrology uses sayana longitudes, whereas followers of Vedic Astrology use the Nirayana system.

An interesting calculation is here to help you understand the impact of Ayanamsa. Approximately 11200 years; hence, the ayanamsa will be exactly the opposite, which means to say, there will be a 180-degree difference between Sidereal and Tropical Astrological System calculations! About 11200 years; if the Sun is positioned in Aries according to the tropical system, the sun will be in Libra, according to Vedic Astrology! Now, that is a big difference, right?

The tropical system superimposes the Zodiac every year on March 21. For western astrology, on March 21st every year, the Sun is always in Aries. The Sidereal system calculates the positions after considering the planets' position behind the Rashi system. These two points differ, resulting in the differences between the predictions made according to your Sun Sign in tropical and Sidereal systems.

The most accepted form of Ayanamsa is the Chitra Paksha ayanamsa proposed by N. C. Lahiri and approved in 1954 by the Astrological Research Institute, Kolkata, India. Most astrologers use this ayanamsa for their calculations. While scholars continue to debate on which is the best and most efficient ayanamsa to follow, as a beginner, you can easily learn about this important element using the Chitra Paksha method.

Here are important terms used in Ayanamsa:

Celestial Latitude - Also called Shar or Vikshep, the celestial latitude is the angular distance of an imaginary arc drawn from the planet to the ecliptic.

Uttarayana - This term refers to the period when Surya enters Makar Rashi and begins his journey towards the north. Uttarayana starts from Makar Sankranti and ends at Mithuna Sankranti. During this period, the duration of daylight time increases with each passing day.

Dakshinayana - This term refers to the period when Surya moves from Karka Sankranti up to Dhanush Sankranti. During the Dakshinayana, the duration of night increases with each passing day.

Equinox - There are two spheres, namely celestial spheres and equators, that intersect each other at 23-degrees, 28-minutes. These two points of intersection are called equinoxes or equinoctial points. One is called the *Vernal Equinox* (Spring Equinox), and the second point of intersection is called *Autumnal* of Fall Equinox.

The Sun revolving in the ecliptic crosses the two celestial spheres twice a year on the equinoxes. On this day, the duration of day and night are equal. The ecliptic changes result in the Sun rising in the northern direction for 6 months (Uttarayana) and in the southern direction for the remaining 6 months (Dakshinayana). As the Sun moves away from the Ayana or from the point of precession, the day's duration increases.

Understanding Dasas

Once you know each of the planets' conditions and strengths, you will know what results you will get from them. But, to know and understand when these results will fructify, you must learn and know about dasas and the transits of the planets through the various Rashis.

So, what are dasas? They are the ruling periods of planets. There are many types of Dasa systems used by astrologers all over. But the most popular, and the most accurate Dasa system is the Vimshottari Dasha System. Let us go into this system in a bit of detail.

You already know that the star constellation in which the moon was passing through becomes your birth Nakshatra. Now, the position and degrees in which this star constellation was placed will determine the dasas that will be in operation right through your lifetime. Here is a chart that details the start of a Dasa, depending on the Nakshatra of your birth. In this chart, we are not considering the movement of the Nakshatra within its 13-degrees, 20-seconds range. The start of the Vimshottari Dasa would have to be adjusted accordingly by reducing the time already passed under the effect of the planet and its lord.

     1. Ashwini Nakshatra - Ketu Dasa - Vimshottari Dasa period is 7 years

     2. Bharani Nakshatra - Venus (Shukra Dasa) - Vimshottari Dasa period is 20 years

     3. Krittika Nakshatra - Sun (Surya Dasa) - Vimshottari Dasa period is 6 years

     4. Rohini Nakshatra - Moon (Chandra Dasa) - Vimshottari Dasa period is 10 years

     5. Mrigashirsha Nakshatra - Mars (Mangala Dasa) - Vimshottari Dasa period is 7 years

     6. Ardra Nakshatra - Rahu Dasa - Vimshottari Dasa period is 18 years

7. Punarvasu Nakshatra - Jupiter (Guru Dasa) - Vimshottari Dasa period is 16 years

8. Pushya Nakshatra - Saturn (Shani Dasa) - Vimshottari Dasa period is 19 years

9. Ashlesha Nakshatra - Mercury (Buddha Dasa) - Vimshottari Dasa period is 17 years

10. Magha Nakshatra - Ketu Dasa - Vimshottari Dasa period is 7 years

11. Purva Phalguni - Venus (Shukra Dasa) - Vimshottari Dasa period is 20 years

12. Uttara Phalguni - Sun (Surya Dasa) - Vimshottari Dasa period is 6 years

13. Hasta - Moon (Chandra Dasa) - Vimshottari Dasa period is 10 years

14. Chitra - Mars (Mangala Dasa) - Vimshottari Dasa period is 7 years

15. Swati - Rahu Dasa - Vimshottari Dasa period is 18 years

16. Vishakha - Jupiter (Guru Dasa) - Vimshottari Dasa period is 16 years

17. Anuradha - Saturn (Shani Dasa) - Vimshottari Dasa period is 19 years

18. Jyeshtha - Mercury (Buddha Dasa) - Vimshottari Dasa period is 17 years

19. Moola - Ketu Dasa - Vimshottari Dasa period is 7 years

20. Purvashada - Venus (Shukra Dasa) - Vimshottari Dasa period is 20 years

21. Uttarashada - Sun (Surya Dasa) - Vimshottari Dasa period is 6 years

22. Shravana - Moon (Chandra Dasa) - Vimshottari Dasa period is 10 years

23. Dhanishta - Mars (Mangala Dasa) - Vimshottari Dasa period is 7 years

24. Satabhisha - Rahu Dasa - Vimshottari Dasa period is 18 years

25. Purva Bhadrapada - Jupiter (Guru Dasa) - Vimshottari Dasa period is 16 years

26. Uttara Bhadrapada - Saturn (Shani Dasa) - Vimshottari Dasa period is 19 years

27. Revati - Mercury (Buddha Dasa) - Vimshottari Dasa period is 17 years

The period of each Dasa is given below:

- Surya Dasa is for 6 years
- Chandra Dasa is for 10 years
- Mangala Mars is for 7 years
- Rahu Dasa is for 18 years
- Guru Dasa is for 16 years
- Shani Dasa is for 19 years
- Buddha Dasa is for 17 years
- Ketu Dasa is for 7 years
- Shukra Dasa is for 20 years

Each of the above is called a *mahadasha*. The Vimshottari Dasa follows a period of 120 years of an individual's life. You likely will not experience all the nine mahadashas in your lifetime. Depending on how many degrees the moon has traveled at your birth time, your first mahadasha is reduced proportionately.

Now, every mahadasha is subdivided into dasas of other planets, and these subdivisions are called antardashas. The first antardasha in every mahadasha is that of the mahadasha planet itself, followed by the other planets in their existing sequence. Each antardashas is further subdivided into Pratyantar Dashas, and this process is repeated until we can arrive at the dasas on a daily and even hourly basis. This book does not cover that detail. This is only to indicate to you the deep detailing found in Vedic Astrology.

While the Vimshottari Dasha System is the most prevalent one, you cannot ignore the other dasa systems. Interestingly, although scientifically, there is an agreement in the way stars and planets are placed in our astral system, there are many differences in terms of Ayanamsas and Dasha Systems. A good and well-trained astrologer can synthesize the interpretations of dasas and by including the ayanamsa aspect of Vedic Astrology.

Chapter 6: The First Four: Aries, Taurus, Gemini, and Cancer

From this chapter onwards until Chapter 8, we will be looking at the Zodiac signs in detail. But before that, let us learn about the categories into which the 12 Zodiac signs fall. The 12 Rashis, along with planets and bhavas or houses, form the fundamental elements of Vedic Astrology.

The literal translation of the word "Rashi" is "piling up". Rashis are not divine, and they are not worshipped like the planets are. They are mystical and yet have a deep connection to earthly elements. If you look at the Rashis or Zodiac Signs symbols, they are fish, the balance, scorpion, and other elements that are part of our earthly life. Nakshatras and planets are divine. They are deities, and they are worshipped.

Even if they are not worshipped and are not divine, the Rashis or Zodiac signs hold deep significance in Vedic Astrology. Rashis are compartments in the sky. They are like an environment. As planets move on their ecliptic, they come into these compartments or Rashis, and depending on the Rashi they enter, the planets behave in a certain way.

One of the basic beliefs of Vedic Astrology is called essential dignity, the idea that the nine planets are more effective and powerful in some signs than in others. This is because of the nature of the planet and the Rashi through which it is transiting through are in harmony. But some planets are weak and have difficult effects while passing through some signs because their natures conflict with each other.

Summarily, the effects of planets in each of these Rashis could be favorable or unfavorable to their natural signification. Here is an analogy to help you understand this concept. Suppose you are a spiritual seeker and suddenly find yourself in a pub playing loud, raucous music; you wouldn't like it, right?

Similarly, if a particular planet finds itself in a Rashi that does not conform to its core principle, then unfavorable effects arise. But if a planet finds itself in Rashi or home aligned with its basic nature, then favorable effects arise. The terms used in Vedic Astrology to explain this concept are exaltation (supportive environment and conforming to the planet's objectives and goals resulting in favorable conditions) and debilitation (non-supportive environment for the planet resulting in unfavorable conditions and effects).

Another important aspect of the 12 Zodiac signs is that each has the opposite, resulting in six opposing couples. Fire and Air are opposites just as Earth and Water are opposites. Here are the six opposing couples:

- Aries (Mesha Rashi) is opposite to Libra (Tula Rashi)
- Cancer (Karkata Rashi) is opposite to Capricorn (Makar Rashi)
- Gemini (Mithuna Rashi) is opposite to Sagittarius (Dhanush Rashi)
- Pisces (Meena Rashi) is opposite to Virgo (Kanya Rashi)
- Taurus (Vrishabha Rashi) is opposite to Scorpio (Vrishchika Rashi)

• Leo (Simha Rashi) is opposite to Aquarius (Kumbha Rashi)

Categories by Flexibility

First, the signs are categorized into three types based on their flexibility. The three types include Movable, Fixed, and Dual.

The first type or movable signs (also called *Cardinal signs*) are Aries, Cancer, Libra, and Capricorn, which represent adaptability, movement, activity, quickness, change, reformation, flexibility, letting go and moving on, and dissatisfaction and restlessness.

The second type of fixed signs is Taurus, Leo, Scorpio, and Aquarius. These four signs represent rigidity, gradual but steady, fixed, headstrong nature, resoluteness, determination, dislike towards movement, and rigid opinions.

The third type of the dual signs (also called *mutable signs*) are Gemini, Virgo, Sagittarius, and Pisces. They are of a dual nature and represent a mix of the first and second types. They are oriented towards learning, philosophical, reading, communication, speech, and preaching. They are open to new ideas and are always exploring different opinions. They are good at multitasking.

Categories by Elements

According to the elements, the 12 Zodiac signs are categorized into four types: earth, fire, wind, and water.

The Fire Signs include Aries, Leo, and Sagittarius. They represent energy, assertion, aggression, passion, willpower, leadership, decisiveness, outspokenness, extroversion, hot temperament, active, drive, pioneering, spontaneous, enthusiastic, and impulsive.

The Earth Signs include Taurus, Virgo, and Capricorn. The earth signs represent practicality, caution, methodical and analytical-based approaches, slow and steady, realistic, down-to-earth, accumulating attitude, love reality more than fiction, understand and appreciate the importance and value of materialistic things. They make great planners, organizers, CEOs, directors, etc.

The Air Signs are Gemini, Libra, and Aquarius. They represent intellect, quick-wittedness, abstract thinking, eager learners, communicative, physically active and agile, love to travel and explore, great social skills, philosophical attitude, and a flexible attitude.

The Water Signs are Cancer, Scorpio, and Pisces. They represent emotion, intuition, learning, passion, sensitiveness, hoarding, and collecting both memories and other non-materialistic things and materials and physical things. They are imaginative, introverts, psychic, secretive, and dreamy. They are not very physically agile. They depend on their intuition more than real facts and evidence.

These elements are also given polarity (positive or negative). Air and fire signs are considered positive, and the earth and water signs are considered negative. So, the following can be arrived at with the Zodiac signs' connections with the four elements and polarity.

Categories by Gender

All odd signs are masculine, which means to say, Aries, Gemini, Leo, Libra, Sagittarius, Aquarius are male. Male signs are more pushy, extroverted, communicative, aggressive, destructive attitudes and negative, dominative, and assertive than female Zodiac signs.

All even signs are feminine; Taurus, Cancer, Virgo, Scorpio, Capricorn, Pisces are female. The feminine Zodiac signs are intuitive, quiet, protective, nurturing, emotional, and gentle.

Other Significant Categorizations

Aries, Scorpio, and Capricorn are considered violent signs. Ruled by Saturn and Mars, they tend to be destructive and primarily have a Tamasic nature. When these signs are afflicted in a native's horoscope, these destructive features will be manifested.

Aries, Gemini, Leo, and Virgo are considered barren signs (concerning female fertility). These planets are not fruitful for conception. But Cancer, Scorpio, and Pisces are believed to be fruitful signs.

Shirsodaya Signs are Gemini, Leo, Virgo, Libra, Scorpio, Aquarius, which means planets in these signs manifest their fruits in the first half of their Dasas. Shirsodaya means "rising the head first."

Pristodaya Signs are Aries, Taurus, Cancer, Sagittarius, Capricorn. Translating to "rising with back," the planets' effects in these signs tend to lead to fruition in the second half of their Dasas.

Ubabodaya Signs (means "rising both sides") is Pisces, which means to say that planets in this sign tend to give their effects in the middle half of their dasas.

Let us look at the first four signs of the Zodiac in detail in this chapter.

Aries - Mesha Rashi

Aries is owned by Mars or Mangala. Aries is the Mooltrikona for Mars, who also owns Scorpio. The symbol of Aries is the ram. Aries is an exaltation sign for Mangala (Mars) and a debilitation sign for Saturn or Shani.

Mental Tendencies of People Born in Aries - Aries is a movable, fire, and masculine sign. People born in this sign are active, bold, fearless, pioneering, charismatic, independent, and inspirational. They make great entrepreneurs, leaders, and businessmen being successful at starting new projects, initiatives, and businesses. They love movement and activity. Their frankness and direct approaches can look confident.

But people born in Aries sign be restless and impatient and find it difficult to sustain energy and interest in their ventures for long periods. They can get aggressive and dominating. Their confidence and frankness could come across as domineering and unpleasant. They are selfish and tend to look only for their own interests more often than not.

Physical Appearance - Individuals born in Mesha Rashi usually have a lean, muscular physique. They have a ruddy complexion with a long neck and face. Their faces are usually broad at the temples and narrow towards the chin. With bushy eyebrows and wiry or rough hair, Aries people often go bald.

Health - Amply supported with the power to resist diseases, Arians typically enjoy good health. They are prone to head injuries that could range from minor to very serious. Them should avoid rash driving. Arians are also likely to suffer from burns, headaches, brain afflictions, inflammatory diseases, pimples, insomnia, and paralysis.

Basic Cautionary Advice - Arians should make sure they get plenty of rest and sleep. They should learn to relax and keep their feelings in exchange, especially anger, worry, and excitement. Stimulants and meat should be avoided while healthy, organic food and vegetables should be included in their daily diets.

Taurus - Vrishabha Rashi

The planet lord of the Taurus sign is Venus. Taurus is a fixed, earth, and feminine sign. The symbol of Taurus is the bull. Taurus is a sign of exaltation for Chandra or the Moon. It is not a debilitation sign for any planet.

Mental Tendencies of People Born Under Taurus Sign - People born in the Taurus Sign are loyal, sensual, down to earth, practical, and stable individuals. They are the kind who believe in slow and steady winning the race. Their determination and perseverance hold them in good stead right through their lives.

They are passionate about and love material possessions. Being conservative, Taureans are highly dedicated and faithful to their home, family, and relationships. They are stubbornly loyal towards their loved ones. Most of the time, they demonstrate a calm and peaceful personality. But they often get agitated when pestered beyond their limits. Taureans can be secretive, violent, unrelenting, and unreasonably stubborn and adamant.

Physical Appearance - Taureans are typically short to average height. They have a broad forehead and are plump with a stout, thick neck. They have a clear complexion, dark hair, and a very well-developed body.

Health - People born under this Rashi usually are blessed with great health and are less sensitive to physical pain than many other people. They rarely admit to physical pains and disability, and if they fall ill, then they have a long and painful recovery period because their recuperative powers are quite low. Taureans are prone to afflictions of the throat and neck.

Basic Cautionary Advice - They should learn not to be overly obstinate. They should work on the slowness of their actions. Being unselfish, non-vindictive, and letting go of anger will also help Taureans lead a happier life than otherwise.

Gemini - Mithuna Rashi

The planet lord owning Gemini or Mithuna Rashi is Mercury or Buddha. Gemini is a dual, air, and masculine sign. The symbol of Gemini is a pair of twins. Mithuna Rashi is a sign of exaltation for Rahu and a sign of debilitation for Ketu.

Mental Tendencies of Gemini-Borns - People born in this sign are communicative, highly intellectual, and do everything, including think, talk, and walk fast. They usually have a pedantic nature and love learning. With excellent writing and reading skills, people of the Gemini sign are clever and versatile. They can multitask well and are adaptable and flexible.

They are witty and bring humor to a group. They love change and diversity, even in their routine life. They can be good in information and data-related fields. But they have different personalities under varied conditions. While their oratory skills are great, they may take on an argumentative approach.

Basic Cautionary Advice - Plenty of rest and sleep is important for Geminis. They should also exercise well, make sure they get fresh air regularly, eat conservatively, and work on building mental peace.

Cancer - Karka Rashi

Chandra or the Moon owns cancer or Karkata Rashi. Cancer is a movable, water, and female sign. Cancer's symbol is the crab and is a sign of exaltation for Guru or Jupiter and a sign of debilitation for Mangala or Mars.

Mental tendencies of Cancerians - People born in the sign of Cancer are emotional, motherly, intuitive, nurturing, and protective. They have excellent memory skills and can save and recall memories of people and objects. With a sympathetic and caring attitude, Cancerians are loved by those around them. Although they love traveling, they do so only if they know they can return to a stable, happy home.

They love domesticated home life and find security in a family environment. They are devoted to their families. They are most hospitable and timid. But they can get aggressive if loved ones are threatened. They have good business instincts, and their ability to learn and imbibe new knowledge is strong. They are honest but are highly impressionable.

Health - They have fragile health during their youth but usually become healthier as they age. They are prone to chest and stomach problems. They must take care of their weakness of being excessively nervous and worried.

Basic Cautionary Advice - They should learn to be patient. Their changing and indolent attitude must be corrected. They should avoid inferiority complexes and become more practical in their life. They should work towards overcoming passiveness, anxiety, and laziness.

Chapter 7: The Middle Earth: Leo, Virgo, Libra, and Scorpio

This chapter deals with the middle four Zodiac signs, namely Leo, Virgo, Libra, and Scorpio. Read on to discover more about each.

Leo - Simha Rashi

The owner of Leo or Simha Rashi is Sun or Surya. Leo is a fixed, fire, and masculine sign. The symbol of Leo is the lion. Simha Rashi is not a sign of exaltation or debilitation for any planet.

Mental tendencies of Leos - People born in this sign have great leadership abilities, are royal, noble, and proud. The Leonines want attention, and they get it; they are as tame as a domestic cat when loved, but can turn into a lion when ignored.

They are outspoken, honest, extroverted, frank, and intense. Leos are confident, independent, and dynamic. They are intelligent and brilliant with great innovative skills. They may be stubborn and ambitious beyond reasonable measure. They love being complimented. They are helpful and have a protective and fatherly attitude towards their friends and loved ones.

Although they are fearless and energetic, they can become pushy in an unpleasantly aggressive way. They are always dogmatic in their approach with others and become annoyingly dominating. Their argumentative nature gets them into trouble with people, especially their superiors and bosses.

Physical Appearance - With broad shoulders, large-sized bones, and muscles, the body of a Leo-born individual usually has a better-formed upper-part than the lower part. Leos have a thin waist and prominent knees. They have soft and wavy hair, although they go bald. A majestic and imposing appearance commands dignity and respect.

Health - Leos have splendid health and rarely fall ill. Even if they do, they recover rapidly from their sickness. But they get alarmed when they become sick or ill, and if the illness is not responding to treatment quickly enough for Leos. The diseases indicated for Leos are heart-related and nerve-related.

Basic Precautionary Advice - Leos should avoid enforcing their opinions and ideas on others and be careful of getting excessively dominating. They should work at taking others' views and suggestions before deciding on any issue. They should hold back their temperamental and hasty nature and remember not to be carried away by flattery.

Virgo - Kanya Rashi

Virgo is the Mooltrikona sign and is owned by Mercury or Buddha, who also owns Gemini. Rahu is also a co-ruler of Virgo. Virgo's symbol is the maiden. Virgo is a dual female sign connected to the earth element. Kanya Rashi is a sign of exaltation for its own lord, namely Mercury, and a sign of debilitation for Shukra or Venus.

Mental Tendencies of Virgo - People born in the Virgo sign are analytical and have a quantitative approach to everything. They are intelligent, deep thinkers, and research-oriented. They are also practical and down to earth. They admire a clean, hygienic, and orderly environment. They are perfectionists and can be quite critical of relentless problems and problematic people. Virgo-born individuals are highly methodical and are ingenious. They are quite precise in their work, although they get nervous and undecided about many things.

They have excellent trade and business instincts. They are good mathematics and are exceedingly orderly and systematic. People born in the Virgo are very hardworking and are continuously striving to do their best. Virgoans lack self-confidence.

Physical Appearance - With dark, curly hair, people born under the Virgo sign usually have a slender body. They have a thin, shrill voice. They walk fast and rarely get a pot-belly. They have a straight nose and, most often, look younger than their real age. They have a pronounced forehead and use honest, frank expressions. Their complexion depends on the ascendant planet and aspects of that planet.

Health - People born under the Virgo sign usually enjoy robust health and live to a ripe, old age. They are active and appear younger than they are, especially in their youth. They are quite particular about their health, too. Virgo-born individuals are prone to stomach and nerve problems.

Basic Precautionary Advice - They should learn to be less talkative and less impulsive, first think before deciding, and be less fickle-minded. They should also learn to forget and forgive others' mistakes. Virgos must avoid discontentment, worries, short temper, and irritability.

Libra - Tula Rashi

Libra is the Mooltrikona sign and is owned by Venus or Shukra, who also owns Taurus. Libra's symbol is the balancing scales. Libra is a male, movable sign related to the air element. Librans are pleasant and balanced. Tula Rashi is a sign of exaltation for Shani or Saturn and a sign of debilitation for Surya or Sun.

Mental Tendencies of Librans - They are very cooperative in a group - as well as social and friendly. Librans are perfectionists and have a deep sense of justice and harmony. They are highly creative, born in the Libra sign, lovers of the arts, including music and literature. They admire the beauty and enjoy social settings. They are courteous and hospitable too.

They are quite charming, diplomatic, and ever-smiling, making them popular and highly likable among many people and friends. They make good judgments of both people and situations quickly. They can be extravagant as they love to live in the lap of luxury. They are excellent at crowd management, have great organizing skills, and might be pushy, though in a pleasant way. Their short-temper may be a big problem for them.

Physical Appearance - With a well-formed body, good complexion, Libras put on weight during their middle age. They have smooth, desirable features, although their body contours and curves can be irregular. They are good-looking, graceful people with an attractive countenance. They look younger than their actual age.

Health - Librans are usually healthy, though they may be prone to infectious diseases. Their Achilles heel in terms of health include kidneys, loins, pineal glands, spinal cord, etc. They should take care of these parts. Diseases indicated for Librans include polyuria, appendicitis, and lumbago.

Basic Cautionary Advice - Librans must learn to control their emotions, especially when they are in a giving mood. They let things go out of hand during such times and give away more than they should. They should learn to say NO to people. Their liberal behavior makes them easy targets for others to take advantage of them.

Scorpio - Vrishchika Rashi

Scorpio or Vrishchika Rashi has two rulers, including Mars or Mangala and Ketu. Scorpio is a fixed, masculine Zodiac sign related to the water element. Scorpio's symbol is the scorpion, the reason why this Rashi is sometimes referred to as "Keeta". Scorpio is not a sign of exaltation for any planet while it is a sign of debilitation for Chandra or Moon.

Mental Tendencies of Scorpions - People born in the Scorpio sign are secretive, passionate, focused, intense, and determined individuals. But they can be obsessive and unyielding, with particularly strong likes & dislikes. Scorpions find it difficult to remain idle, and they work best when faced with hurdles and obstacles. They never surrender and fight to the end.

They may be outwardly calm even when undergoing inner turmoil, thanks to their strong emotions and complex imaginative skills. They are moody and temperamental and do not forget and forgive easily. They can be good friends but also be the worst enemy. Therefore, they never have lifelong friends.

They are quite cunning and excellent detectives, considering their ability to hide their true emotions and personality. They also have good psychic skills. However, they get quite jealous and cling on to revengeful feelings. Although they are stubborn, people born in Scorpio are charismatic and self-made individuals.

Interestingly, the Scorpio sign represents two types - the higher type with great control over their senses and the lower type of Scorpios who are rude, jealous, and irreconcilable seekers of materialistic pleasure.

Physical Appearance - With a well-proportioned body, Scorpions generally are good-looking. They are average stature, broad, and a commanding presence. They usually gravitate towards being stout and are typically square-faced. Most are of dusky complexion unless their ascendant is affected by a malefic planet(s).

Health - Diseases and problems for Scorpions are found in the bladder, pelvic bone, prostate glands, seminal vesicles, and others. They could be affected by brain afflictions, coma, neuralgia, insomnia, and somnambulism.

Basic Precautionary Advice - Scorpions need to control their sarcasm and overly critical attitude. They should avoid selfishness and secret animosity. The negative aspect of Scorpio is its ability to create anarchy and destruction. It is best to know this failing and work towards avoiding your personality to take on these habits.

Chapter 8: The Heaven Above: Sagittarius, Capricorn, Aquarius, and Pisces

This chapter deals with the final four signs of the Zodiac. Read on to discover more about these four.

Sagittarius - Dhanush Rashi

Sagittarius or Dhanush Rashi is owned by Jupiter or Guru, who also owns Pisces. Sagittarius' Mooltrikona is Sagittarius. The symbol of Sagittarius is the archer, and sometimes, the Centaur represents it. Dhanush Rashi is a sign of exaltation for Ketu and a sign of debilitation for Rahu.

Mental Tendencies of Sagittarius - Sagittarius is a dual, masculine sign connected to the fire element. People born in the Sagittarius sign are outspoken, bold, and optimistic individuals. They can look at the positive side of all things, regardless of how tough or difficult a situation might be. They are best when faced with hurdles and obstacles. They are blessed with an abundance of vigor, vitality, energy, and enthusiasm.

They are idealistic in their outlook and love traveling. They are attracted to spirituality and religion and have strong faith. They are determined and even pushy to an extent. But they are very jovial, just, and friendly people. They can put on a business-like behavior, although they end up promising more than they can deliver.

Their communication style is expansive and outspoken. They can be blunt to a fault. They love to preach and teach and do well in the fields of law. medicine, teaching, and religion.

Physical Appearance - With a well-developed and well-proportioned physique, people born under the Sagittarius sign are tall and slender with either a long or an oval face. They have a large forehead and bushy or high eyebrows. They have expressive eyes and a charming presence. They bald early, especially near the temples.

Health - The body parts about health and diseases are thighs, hips, buttocks, etc. Therefore, diseases indicated are hip fractures, rheumatism, gout, lung troubles, etc.

Basic Precautionary Advice - Sagittarians should be careful not to hurt or insult others with their overly frank and outspoken way of communicating. It is not important that they do not develop enmity towards their parents and siblings. They are likely to fail at the home front and not get the independence they seek in their domestic life. So, adjustment would be required. It is also necessary not to exaggerate and talk non-stop using lies, undeliverable promises, and to insult or hurt others.

Capricorn - Makar Rashi

Saturn or Shani owns Capricorn or Makar Rashi. Capricorn is a movable female sign connected to the earth element. Capricorn's symbol is the goat. Capricorn is a sign of exaltation for Mangala or Mars and a sign of debilitation for Guru or Jupiter.

Mental Tendencies of Capricorn-Born Individuals - People born in Capricorn are practical, prudent, intelligent, and down-to-earth individuals. They are serious, orthodox, and reserved people. They are very methodical and persistently plod through their tasks.

They love to travel. With their high levels of perseverance, they rise to the top slowly but steadily and become self-made individuals. They have keen business skills, organizational skills, and managerial ability. Capricorn people are thoughtful, patient, and tolerant of others. They do not trust those around them easily. They are capricious and desirous of power, authority, and wealth.

Physical Appearance - With a prominent, long, and thin nose, people born in the sign of Capricorn are commonly short at their young age but become tall suddenly after 16 years. They are likely to become hunch-backed with advancing age. They usually have a defect while walking.

Basic Precautionary Advice - They must learn not to be very pessimistic, egoistic, and selfish. They should learn not to become broken-hearted or desperate. Avoid overworking and take rest to maintain physical and mental health. The people born in this sign should be careful not to get carried away by discontentment and undue nervousness.

Aquarius - Kumbh Rashi

Aquarius or Kumbh Rashi is owned by Shani, for whom this is the Mooltrikona too. Also, Rahu is the co-ruler of Aquarius. The symbol of Aquarius is the water-bearer. Aquarius is a fixed, masculine Zodiac sign representing the air element. Kumbh Rashi is not a sign of exaltation or debilitation for any planet.

Mental Tendencies of Kumbh Rashi Individuals - People born in the Aquarius sign are abstract thinkers. They are socially conscious individuals. Like the people born in Capricorn, those born in Aquarius are also serious and thoughtful but are more communicative. They are stubborn and are rigid in thinking. They do not like moving and changing situations. They have a scientific and research-oriented bent of mind. They are hard workers with excellent organization skills.

They are extraordinarily intelligent and inventive and can think ahead of time. They are creative and make friends easily, but have strong likes and dislikes. They are highly altruistic and unselfish. They are also rebellious and love to preach about change, although they themselves are resistant to changes of any kind. They have great self-control too. They have strong, innovative ideas and are self-thinking individuals. They can be stubborn, but they are not foolhardy.

Physical Appearance - People born in this sign generally have a tall stature. They have a well-developed, strong physique and become a bit stout during their middle years. But they have a handsome, pleasing personality.

Health - Kumbh Rashi people are highly susceptible to infectious diseases. They could also have heart-related afflictions, including rheumatism and blood pressure.

Basic Precautionary Advice - If any other planet's adverse aspect afflicts the ascendant planet or Saturn, then the native is likely to be lazy and lethargic. Such people should cultivate hard work and be active and prompt. They should not be alone and worry excessively. Avoid pessimism and gloominess. They should also take care of being unreasonably rigid about their likes and dislikes.

Pisces - Meena Rashi

Jupiter owns Pisces or Meena Rashi. Pisces is a dual, feminine sign connected to the water element. Pisces' symbol is the fish. The Pisces sign is a sign of exaltation for Venus or Shukra and a sign of debilitation for Mercury or Buddha.

Mental Tendencies of Pisces-Born Individuals - People born in the Pisces sign are emotional, sensitive, and quite impressionable. Pisceans tend to be dreamy and romantic with a kind, charitable, and a giving and forgiving attitude. They are fond of music and arts and are somewhat disconnected from reality. They are weak in physical and mental activity and trust others easily. They are philosophical and have a passionate attitude towards life.

They can be moody and temperamental and yet have a spiritual and meditative approach to life and its problems. They like being alone and often get into a reflective mood. They are forgetful and have a tendency to have dreams and psychic visions. They are friendly and softly magnetic and have a happy-go-lucky attitude. They have a liberal outlook, but lack confidence and determination. They may get indecisive to that extent.

Physical Appearance - Pisceans usually have a plump body and a short stature. They have a fleshy face and a tendency for a double chin. Their shoulders are spherical and muscular.

Health - Pisceans could be addicted to drinking. Health indicators for them include gastric troubles and varicose veins. Liver and feet afflictions are also indicated.

Basic Precautionary Advice - Pisceans are easily impressed, and therefore, they could end up befriending people putting up pretenses, thus harming themselves. So, it is important for individuals born in the sign of Pisces to take care and be choosy while making friends. Pisceans also need to learn to be pushy. They can be generous but should be warned about being overly liberal.

Chapter 9: Divisional Charts

Now that you have the basics of planets, stars, and Rashis in place, we can move on to predictive astrology using a unique technique of Vedic Astrology called *Divisional Charts*. The credit of the success to make accurate predictions is largely contributed by these Divisional Charts, which are also known as *Varga Charts*.

Varga is a Sanskrit term meaning "division" called a *Zodiac sign or Rashi division*. Each division or fractional part is called an *"amsa"*. Here is a simple explanation for you. You already know that each Zodiac sign has 30-degrees in its space. In these charts, this sign of 30-degrees is further subdivided into different numbers of equal divisions or amsas.

Each planet is again mapped in each of these amsas resulting in Divisional Charts of a native. Each amsa has an influence on the native's life. Vedic Astrology uses 16 Vargas or divisional charts resulting in a unique system to find the auspicious and inauspicious effects of planets.

The Parashara System of Astrology uses these 16 divisional charts for predictive astrology. In the Rashi chart, the 12 regions correspond to the 12 Zodiac signs. If there are two divisions, then it means each house or regions is divided into two amsas or parts, resulting in 24 regions. And this goes on.

- **The Rashi Chart** (only one division) called *D1* is used to predict details about the native's physical matters, including his body, status of health, and other general matters. The Rashi Chart is the basic one where the study of a native's horoscope begins.

- **The Hora Chart** (with 2 divisions) called *D2* deals with wealth and family. The D2 helps to understand the financial position and matters of the native. A strong position of the Sun in this chart means the quantity of wealth owned by the native will be very good. If the Moon has a strong position, earning money will be easy for the native.

- **The Drekkana Chart** (with three divisions) dealing with siblings and the nature of the native is called *D3*. Planets in certain divisions of this chart can bode badly. For example, if planets are in the Sarpa Drekkana, then it is not considered good for the native's health condition.

- **The Chaturthamsa Chart** (with four divisions) called *D4* deals with matters relating to fortune and property.

- **The Saptamsa Chart** (with seven divisions) called *D7* deals with the aspects of children and progeny.

- **The Navamsa Chart** (with nine divisions) called *D9* is used to predict the spouse (or wife), dharma, and the relationships of the concerned native. After the Rashi Chart, the Navamsa Chart is the most important one used in predictive Vedic Astrology. If a planet is exalted in the Rashi Chart but debilitated in D9, then the planet may not be beneficial. Interestingly, the lord of the 64th division in D9 is an indicator of longevity and Marala Dasa (connected to death) of the native.

- **The Dasamsa Chart** (with ten divisions) called *D10* deals with the native's profession and his or her interactions in society.

- **Dvadamsa Chart** (with 12 divisions) or *D12* deals with parents

- **Shodasamsa Chart** (with 16 divisions) or *D16* is for traveling, vehicles, and comforts.

- **Vimsamsa Chart** (with 20 divisions) or *D20* is for spiritual pursuits.

- **Chatur Vimsamsa Chart** (with 24 divisions) or *D24* is for education, knowledge, and learning.

- **Sapta Vimsamsa Chart** (with 27 divisions) or *D27* is for the strengths and weaknesses of the native.

- **Trimsamsa Chart** (with 30 divisions) or *D30* is for evils, bad luck, and failures.

- **Khavedamsha Chart** (with 40 divisions) or *D40* 0s for maternal legacy.

- **Akshavedamsa Chart** (with 45 divisions) or *D45* is for paternal legacy.

- **Shastiamsa Chart** (with 60 divisions) or *D60* is for part births and karma

Besides the above 16 Vargas attributed to Parashara, there are four more attributed to Jaimini. These four Vargas or divisional charts include:

1. **Panchamsa** (with five divisions) is called *D5* and represents fame and power.

2. **Shasthamsa** (with six divisions) is called *D6*, which represents health.

3. **Ashtamsa** (with eight divisions), or *D8* representing unexpected troubles.

4. **Ekadasamsa or Rudramsa** (with 11 divisions) representing death and destruction.

The biggest challenge in drawing up such detailed divisional charts is that the exact time of a person's birth is rarely obtained. Even a minute difference in noting the time of birth could affect the accuracy. The accurate time of birth is essential because otherwise, the Lagna and other planetary positions can change significantly, resulting in wrong the charts being used to make predictions. But there are cases, especially when the father is a doctor and attended the birth, when correct times of birth have been recorded. Then it is possible to create precise charts for the native.

Of all the above charts, the Rashi Chart is the primary, and all the other divisional charts and information received from them relate to this. For example, if Jupiter is in the Mool Trikona in the Rashi chart and it is in a sign of debilitation in D10 or the Dasamsa chart, which deals with the native's profession and career. The debilitated Jupiter should give you an indication that the native could be a bad boss whom people fear and hate at his or her workplace. The 10th house and the lord of the 10th house in the D10 chart is important for career-related predictions.

In all the divisional charts, the Kendra houses are the most important ones. If the Kendra houses have good planets in them, then the native's career is likely to do well. So, analyzing the Rashi chart will give you inputs about the native's profession or career, while the analysis of the D10 will give you insights into the progress and quality.

Continuing further, the benefic planets are depending on the Lagna. So, for a correct and full analysis of a native's career, you would need to check the Lagna, the Sun and Moon positions, and the 10th house from the Lagna. The same procedure should be used for accurate predictions of other aspects of a native's life using the other divisional charts.

Planets become increasingly benefic and auspicious if they occupy the same Zodiac house in the 16 divisional charts. The planets get graded based on this element. If a planet is stationed in its own sign or the Mooltrikona sign or in any other good sign in two of the 16 Vargas, it is said to have achieved Parijat Amsa.

If the planet acquires this condition in any three divisional charts, it is said to have achieved Uttam Amsa. This gradation of a planet increases with the number of Vargas with this condition, and the status names for each planet are:

- In four Vargas - Gopuramsa
- In five Vargas - Simhasana amsa
- In six Vargas - Paravatmasa
- In seven Vargas - Devlok amsa
- In eight Vargas - Kumkumamsa
- In nine Vargas - Iravatamsa
- In ten Vargas - Vaishnavamsa
- In 11 Vargas - Saivamsa
- In 12 Vargas - Bhaswadansa
- In 13 Vargas - Vaisheshikamsa
- In 14 Vargas - Indrasanamsa
- In 15 Vargas - Golokamsa
- In 16 Vargas - Shrivallabhamsa

Implication and Importance of Divisional Charts

Divisional charts are essential for a detailed analysis of any horoscope. One of the primary purposes is to note the placement of a planet in different charts. If a particular planet is in a strong position in many divisions, then it is strong. If it is in weak places, then the planet is rendered weak.

A planet located in one Zodiac sign or Rashi by itself is called a *"yoga"* or an *"avayoga"* because of the relationship the planet establishes with the lord of that Rashi as well as the lords of the other related Rashis, especially in connection with Lagna. It is important to note that the mere occupation of a planet in a Rashi will not produce the results or effects in accordance with that occupation.

This is because no planet can act alone. Every planet establishes active relationships with one or more other planets and the Rashi it occupies, and Varga-wise status gained by the planet and multiple other factors. If a yoga fails to give the expected result, then the reason could be anything. For example, it could be the Varga-wise weakness of the planet rather than the planet itself.

Let us take an example to understand this concept. The Sun in the 9th house not in any hostile sign gives wealth, friends, piety, and children to the native, although this position can drive antagonism towards the father and wife, having reduced happiness. If the Sun is the Lagna lord and is in the exalted 9th house, then the native and his father could have a great relationship, and there need not be any reduction in happy times. So, the expected negative results are counted by other factors as defined from the divisional charts.

Following are more examples of using Divisional Charts for predictions.

Planets in Navamsa Affecting Future Life - The Navamsa chart or D9 represents spouse and marriage and the dignity of planets. This chart must be consulted for matters related to marriage, besides its being one of the most important divisional charts used for other predictions. D9 is important because it is seen as the fruit if D1 or the Rashi chart is the tree. The Navamsa signifies the authentic dignity of a planet because it stands for the planets giving their effects or fruits through its Dasas.

From a philosophical context, D9 represents the thought process the native would develop after he or she experiences life and learns from these events. There arises the concept of D9 triggering future life, or at least later in the current dasa. And the same logic supports the idea that a planet in a strong position in D9 is bound to give better results later in time or later during its dasa. The Navamsa will depict your learning from the life lessons the planet offered you.

Another key element to remember is that the idea of exaltation and debilitation signs are more significant in D1 than in any other divisional chart. According to Sage Parashara, the exaltation or debilitation signs and specific degrees are clearly defined. For example, Chandra is exalted in the 2nd pada of Krittika, which is the first Navamsa of Taurus. In the 2nd Navamsa of Taurus becomes the Mooltrikona of Chandra.

In Navamsa or any other divisional chart, the second pada of Krittika does not fall after the first pada of Krittika. So, with exaltation and debilitation, the lengths or degrees become immaterial. Only the D1 should be considered for this aspect. Therefore, in this particular case, Chandra in the second pada of Krittika will not result in anything bad in later life or in the later part of Chandra Dasa.

Another point of interest is that if a planet is weak in the Rashi Chart, its position is not improved significantly, even if it is in a solid position in any of the divisional charts. The reverse is, but different. If a planet is in a strong position, its strength is reduced if it is placed in a position of debilitation in the Divisional Chart under consideration.

Here is an example to illustrate this. Suppose your Rashi Chart has the lord of the 10th house in an exalted position. If the concerned astrologer has predicted good fortune in your career based on this without checking the relevant divisional chart, then this prediction may not come true. Maybe the same planet is in a debilitation sign in the D10 (divisional career chart). So, correct predictions, in this case, can be obtained only by checking and verifying both the D1 and D10 charts.

In summary, we can say this about Divisional Charts. The Rashi Charts are like the human body, which gives you a general understanding of a person's life. If you want detailed ways of how the internal systems are working, you would have to do ECG or biopsy or other tests concerned with that particular part, right? The Divisional Charts are like these detailed studies that give you information about specific areas of your life.

Chapter 10: Planetary Strengths and Avasthas

After Divisional Charts, we will focus on another powerful predictive technique used in Vedic Astrology, namely Planetary Strengths. The various longitudinal-based positioning of the planets combined with a concept called "*six-fold strength*" is a powerful tool used for higher prediction levels.

Let us start by understanding what *avastha* is. It is an important concept in the world of Vedic Astrology. Avastha in Sanskrit translates to "stage," "state," or "level." It refers to the state or stage of planets. There are many types of avasthas, the most basic one highly useful for beginners being the "Baladi Avastha".

In the odd Zodiac signs, namely Aries, Gemini, Leo, Libra, Sagittarius, and Aquarius, any planet is in the following avasthas according to the degrees:

- 0-6 degrees - The planet is said to be in its infancy avastha, during which time it will have minimal effects on the native.

- 6-12 degrees - The planet is said to be in adolescence avastha, and during this period, its entire potential effects can be experienced.

- 12-18 degrees - In this mature state, the planet will render its full potential.

- 18-24 degrees - In this old stage, the planet will have limited effects.

- 24-30 degrees - During the last 6-degrees of a Zodiac (near-death state), the planet will have very minimal effects, if any.

In the even Zodiac signs, namely Taurus, Cancer, Virgo, Scorpio, Capricorn, and Pisces, the planets are in the following avasthas as per the longitudinal degrees:

- 0-6 degrees - Near-death avastha
- 6-12 degrees - Old avastha
- 12-18 degrees - mature avastha
- 18-24 degrees - adolescent avastha
- 24-30 degrees - near-death avastha

These degree measurements mustn't be taken literally but considered liberally. According to degrees, this differentiation implies that planets somewhat in the center of a Zodiac sign (between 12 - 18 degrees) render their maximum effects. A planet towards the ends of the signs tend to blend into the next or previous sign and is not very deeply colored by the current Rashi. From a mathematical perspective, the 15-degrees point is at the dead center of a sign, and is most affected by the characteristics of that sign.

Significance of Residential Strength of a Planet

Every horoscope has a rising sign called the Lagna or the ascendant. It is one of the 12 Zodiac signs, of course. But, according to the precise time of birth, the Lagna will have an exact degree within that sign between 0 and 30. This degree becomes an important point of every sign for that native's horoscope.

Let us take an example. Suppose the ascendant sign is Capricorn at 20-degrees for a person. This 2nd house for this person would be Aquarius. The 20th degree of the second house will be the exact center of the 2nd bhaav, which represents speech, family, wealth, money, etc.

A planet in any sign at exactly 20-degrees of a house will have 100% of residential strength and give its full potential of effects. The strength of the bhaav will be good between 15 and 25 degrees (plus or minus 5 degrees). Beyond this limit, the bhaav of that sign will decrease with every degree away from 20-degrees.

In the same example, if a planet is at 4-degrees of a particular sign, according to the Baladi Avastha, it belongs to the previous sign. For example, if a planet is at 2 degrees in Aquarius (the 2nd sign), then although it is in the 2nd house, the bhaav of the previous sign will be in effect.

Significance of Nakshatra Placement

To reiterate, there are 12 Zodiac signs of 30-degrees each and 27 Nakshatras or asterisms of 13-degrees, 20-minutes each. These 27 Nakshatras are ruled by the nine planets, namely Ketu, Shukra, Surya, Chandra, Mangala, Rasu, Guru, Shani, and Buddha (the first nine asterisms respectively). The same sequence of planet lords is then maintained for the next 9 Nakshatras, and again for the third set of nine Nakshatras.

The above situation means every one of the nine planets rules over three Nakshatras equidistant from each other. You already know that the Nakshatra in which the Moon is housed at the time of a person's birth becomes the birth Nakshatra of the native. Planets in the 3rd, 5th, and 7th Nakshatras from the birth Nakshatra of a person will be weak and give malefic effects to him or her. Planets in the 2nd, 6th, and 9th asterisms will give beneficial effects, and the planets in the 1st, 4th, and 8th asterisms will be neutral, although slightly skewed towards giving positive effects for the native in question.

Significance of Planetary Strengths in Varga Charts

Sage Parashara, in addition to defining the 16 Varga Charts, also gave a weighted scheme to attribute the importance of these charts to analyze horoscopes and make predictions. This weighted scheme is useful to obtain a quantitative analysis of the effects of the planets using scores for each planet obtained through this scheme. Higher the score of a planet, the better the results of that particular in its Vimshottari Dasa. High scores reflect the fructification powers of the planet under consideration.

The weighted scheme given by Sage Parashara uses only six of the 16 divisional charts and is:

1. Rashi Chart (D1) - 6 points
2. Hora Chart (D2) - 2 points
3. Drekkana Chart (D3) - 4 points
4. Navamsa Chart (D9) - 5 points
5. Dwadasamsa Chart (D12) - 2 points
6. Trimsamsa Chart (D30) - 1 point

Every planet has a total potential score of 20 points. To reiterate, the exaltation and debilitation effects of planets in divisional charts do not hold value. The following sequence of houses denotes the decreasing value of beneficial effects offered by any planet:

1. Mooltrikona house
2. Own house
3. Best friend house
4. Friend house
5. Neutral house
6. Enemy house
7. Great enemy house

Sage Parashara also defined the weightage for each of the above placements of planets. Let us use an example to illustrate this weightage scheme used in Vedic Astrology. Suppose Mooltrikona is 100%, 90% to own house, and so forth. Next, suppose a planet is housed in the Mooltrikona in D1 and its own house in D9, in the house of a best friend in another divisional chart, and so forth. Then, the weightage scheme looks like this: 100% of 6 + 90% of 5 +........... (similar contributions from the other six divisional charts to be filled here) to take the total score out of 20.

This total from the weightage scheme will give you a numeric value, which is a good indicator of how the planet will behave in its Vimshottari Dasa. The reason for Sage Parashara to use this weightage scheme is quite evident. As you already know, the Varga charts represent the different aspects of our life. For example, D1 gives a general outlook on a native's life, D9 is for marriage and spouse, D3 is for siblings, D10 is for career, etc. all of which are the support systems of our life. So, the planet's position reflects the depth and level of these support systems. The better the numerical score, the better the beneficial effects of that planet.

Shadbala - The Six-Fold Strength in Vedic Astrology

Any planet or *Graha* gets strength from various sources, including the Rashi, Varga, Bhava, Day or nighttime, Krishna/Shukla Paksha, and more. Krishna Paksha is the fortnight that starts from the full moon day (Poornima) to the new moon day (Amavasya). Shukla Paksha is the other fortnight that starts from the new moon day until the full moon day.

Shadbala is a mathematical system used to quantify the strength of a planet attained through six sources. This number representing the strength of a planet is an important tool to understand the real impact of the concerned planet on the different aspects of a native's life. Detailed and extensive explanations of assessing a planet's strength are given in the Brihat Parashara Hora Shastras. The unit of strength is measured in Virupas.

The mathematical computation given by Sage Parashara is quite complex and layered. But most experienced astrologers can quickly assess the strength of a planet by making a mental model. Let us look at the six sources of strength used in Shadbala.

- **Sthana Bala** - The strength of a planet drawn from the various positions and stations it takes in the Rashi Chart and other Varga charts are called *Sthana Bala* or strength from the occupied place.

- **Dik Bala** - This source of strength of a planet is drawn from its placements in specific Kendras.

- **Kala Bala** - The strength of a planet that depends on the time of an event or the birth of a person is called Kalabala.

- **Chesta Bala** - The strength drawn from the movement of the planet is called *Chestbala*. The movement of a planet means whether it is moving fast, slow, forward, or reverse.

- **Naisargika Bala** - This source of strength is depending on the natural power (or strengths) and weakness of a planet.

- **Drgbala** - The strength drawn from the malefic and benefic planet is called *drgbala*. The benefic planets (or shubh grahas) are sources of strength, whereas a malefic planet (or papa Graha) is a source of weakness.

Let us look at each strength in detail.

Sthana Bala or the Positional Strength of a Planet

The Sthana Bala of a planet is based on its "placement" or "position" as explained above and represents the "place" factor. "Sthana" in Sanskrit translates to "place". The maximum Sthana Bala strength a planet can achieve is 390 Virupas comprising of the strengths derived from the six components discussed below:

1. **Uccha Bala** - This position indicates the distance of the planet from its deepest exaltation point. The closer is this distance, the stronger the effects of the planet. Maximum strength - 30 virupas

2. **Saptavargaja Bala** - This indicates the power of a planet in seven divisional charts, including the Rashi Hora Drekkana Saptamsa, Navamsa, Dwadasamsa, and Trimvimsa. Maximum strength - 225 Virupas

3. **Ojayuggama Bala** - Oja translates to male or odd, and yumna means female or even. This type of Sthana bala is sourced from male and female planets placed in male and female Zodiac Signs. Female planets in female signs and male planets in male signs get this source of strength. A male planet in a female sign or a female planet in a male sign do not derive this strength. Maximum strength - 30 virupas

4. **Kendradi Bala** - The 1, 4, 7, and 10 bhaavs or houses are collectively known as Kendra. The 2nd, 5th, 8th, and 11th are known as Succedent or panapara. The 3rd, 6th, 9th, and 12th are known as precedent houses or apoklima. Planets in

the Kendra are the strongest, and those in the apoklima are the weakest. The planets placed in the panapara houses are of middling strength. Maximum strength - 60 virupas

5. **Drekkana Bala** - The male planets, namely Sun, Mars, and Jupiter, get their full strength in the 1st drekkana (the house of the sign itself). The female planets, namely Moon and Venus, get their full strength in the 2nd Drekkana (5th house from the Rashi). The eunuch planets, namely Mercury and Mars, get their full strength in the 3rd drekkana (the 9th house) of a Rashi or house. Maximum strength - 15 virupas.

From the above discussion, it is clear that if a planet achieves the maximum Saptavargaja bala, then the quantum of other Sthana bala becomes insignificant.

Dik Bala - the Directional Strength

This type of planetary strength is derived from the four Kendras, which represent the four directions or Dik. Lagna represents the East. Jupiter and Mercury get their Dik bala here. The 7th house from Lagna represents the West. Shani gets dik bala in this house. The 10th house represents the South. Mars and Sun get their dik bala in the 10th house. The 4th house represents the North where the Moon and Venus get their dik bala.

And the elements or tattva ruling the Lagna are the Akasha (ether) and Prithvi (earth). The element ruling the 4th house is Jala (water), that ruling the 7th house is Vayu (wind), and that ruling the 10th house is Agni (fire). When planets are in their dik balas, then the tattva lording over these houses also gets great prominence and strength, resulting in the native being blessed by the tattva devata.

Kala Bala - the Time Strength

This type of planetary strength depends on the time, such as hours, day, night, fortnight, month, year, etc. Each planet is strong at points in time and weak at other times. The maximum strength that can be achieved through Kala bala is 390 virupas. There are five components to Kala bala, including:

    1. Natonnata Bala - This type of strength is based on day or night. Some planets are strong at night, and some are strong during the day. Sun, Jupiter, and Venus are strongest at noon. Moon, Mars, and Shani are strongest at midnight. Mercury is strong right through the day. Maximum strength - 60 virupas

    2. Tribhaga Bala - In this type, day and night are each divided into 3 parts. Then, six planets (excluding Jupiter) get their maximum strength at different portions of day and night. Mercury, Sun, and Saturn are strong in the first, second, and third positions of the day, respectively. Moon, Venus, and Mars are strong in the first, second, and third portions of the night, respectively. Jupiter is strong through all the six portions. Maximum strength - 60 virupas

    3. Paksha Bala - Some planets are strong during Krishna Paksha, while others are strong during Shukla Paksha. The benefic planets or shubh Grahas Chandra, Mercury, Jupiter, and Venus are strongest during Poornima. The malefic planets are strongest during Amavasya. Maximum strength - 60 virupas.

    4. Varsha-Maas-Dina-Hora Bala - Different planets rule various time segments. It starts with the ruler of the year (Abda - solar year), which is subdivided into four components, namely month (Maas - solar month), week (Vara or Dina - Vedic weekday), and hour (hora - graha hour). Each of these four components is stronger than the previous one by 25%, making the Hora lord the strongest of the four. Vara Lord, which is the second strongest, is the Hora Lord at sunrise. Masa Lord, the third strongest, is the Hora Lord during the transit of the Sun from one Zodiac sign to the next. Abda Lord, the weakest of the four components, is the Hora Lord now when the Sun enters Aries. - Maximum strength - 150 virupas.

5. **Ayana Bala** - This source of Kala Bala depends on the movements of the planets in the Uttarayana or Dakshinayana directions. Maximum strength - 60 virupas.

Chesta Bala - Strength from the Motion of Planets

Chesta in Sanskrit translates to "effort", and the source of Chesta bala is determined by the efforts or movements made by planets. A planet that moves steadily is considered making fewer efforts, and when moving in retrograde, it is considered making a maximum effort. A retrograde movement can be compared to the movement against a flowing current, which requires a lot of effort.

The Sun and Moon always move steadily with no acceleration or retrogression. For planets Mercury to Saturn, Chesta Bala is calculated on the direction and speed of their movements. Calculating the Chest Bala of a planet uses a complex mathematical computation. There are eight different movements and their strengths defined in Vedic Astrology.

1. **Vakra** - Moving in reverse or retrogression - 100% strength, a planet's full brilliance is demonstrated at this strength.

2. **Anuvakra** - Moving to the previous Rashi when in retrogression - 60% strength

3. **Vikala** - No movement; the planet is standing still - 15% strength

4. **Manda** - Slow-moving, decelerating planet - 30% strength

5. **Mandatara** - Moving very slowly and appearing as if not moving at all - 15% strength

6. **Sama** - Slow acceleration - 7.5% strength

7. **Chara** - Moving in the forward direction at average speed - 45% strength

8. **Atichara** - Moving in the forward direction with above-average speed - 30% strength

Naisargika Bala - the Natural Strength

The natural strength of planets is called *Naisargika Bala*. Planets get progressively stronger in the following list:

- Saturn
- Mars
- Mercury
- Jupiter
- Venus
- Moon
- Sun

When two planets are positioned to mutually influence each other, then the stronger planet influences the weaker ones and predominantly produces its effects. From the above list, the Sun is the strongest planet. When any planet is in conjunction with the Sun, then it becomes combust. The Naisargika Bala of the Sun, while in conjunction with other planets, will never reduce.

Drgbala - the Aspect Strength

Drgbala is derived from being the natural aspect of the planet, whether naturally malefic or benefic. The aspect of natural malefic reduces the strength of the planet, while the aspect of natural benefic enhances its strength. The aspect's strength depends on the longitudinal difference between the aspected planet and the aspecting planet.

A naturally benefic planet (Venus, Jupiter, benefic Buddha, and the waxing Moon) aspects another planet, then it enhances the strength of the aspected planet. Contrarily, when naturally malefic planets (Mars, Saturn, Surya, Malefic Mercury, and the waning Moon) aspect a planet, then the aspected planet's strength is reduced.

Again, computing the Drgbala of a planet is complex and time-consuming. Most astrologers use a commonly accepted approximation method, which does cause a small error that can be ignored.

While it might be impractical to arrive at the strength of a planet mathematically (considering the complex computation usually involved), it is possible to arrive at accurate predictions based on understanding the conditions that render planets power. It is not necessary to know the complete, complex computation processes to know the strength and the corresponding effects of a planet. A proper understanding of the six-fold strength concept is sufficient. At this juncture, it makes sense to speak about Chandra's special power or strength, the Moon, considering this planet is seen as the natural sustainer and nurturer of a horoscope. The waxing and waning period of the Moon also affects its strength.

For Chandra, Paksha Bala is more important than Sthana Bala. Therefore, even if Chandra occupies a place that weakens its strength, but is strong because of Paksha Bala, then Chandra is considered strong. And if Chandra is placed in a strong position in a horoscope, the other planets' strength gets positively affected, as the Moon lends its power to the others. All the benefic planets acquire their strength during Chandra's Shukla Paksha. So, the more strength Chandra has in its Paksha Bala, the more power the benefic planets get.

Chapter 11: Timing of Events: Dashas and Transits

Astrology is all about timing future events and making accurate predictions. The Rashi Chart or birth chart of a native gives you an insight into the inherent promise held in his or her life based on the positions of the planets and other considerations connected to the planets, Rashis, etc. It only shows you the inherent promise that the life of the concerned native holds. But, when this promise can turn to fruition depends on elements called Dashas and the movement/transits of planets.

You have read and learned about the Dasa period of each planet. The total Dasa period of a planet or Graha is divided into multiple parts, which are, in turn, ruled by different planets and their lords. The Dasa that is operative, and the corresponding results involve various factors, including the natural signification of the planet, its ruler, its position and placement, aspects, and the strength.

The Dasa's major period is called the *mahadasha*, subdivided into smaller periods in which all the nine planets are operative within the mahadasha of a planet. The transit of planets, especially Shani and Guru, plays a crucial role in any important event happening in the lifetime of a native.

For example, Shani Mahadasha will have antardashas (sub-periods) within its 19-year duration. For instance, Shukra will be an antardasha within the Shani Mahadasha for 2 years and 9 months. So, during this period, the effects of Shani Mahadasha, along with Venus antardasha, should be analyzed for accurate predictions. During the 2years 9 months period of Venus antardasha, you must know what both Shani and Venus are doing in the Zodiac sky.

The promise when the effects of good karma fructify will depend on the Dasa and the planets' transit through the Dasa. Let us discuss important events that can be accurately predicted based on the birth chart, Dasas, and planets' transit. We will use examples to learn about the topics of this chapter.

Case Study I

Date of Birth - 13th December 1956; Time of Birth - 11:10 pm; Place of Birth - Delhi

When this person was born, the balance of Ketu Dasa happening at the time (calculated from the time of the native's birth) was 3 years, 11 months, and 1 day. Using this information, the Vimshottari Dasa of a person born on the above date, time, and place will be:

- Ketu Dasa (Balance remaining) - up to four years of age
- Shukra Dasa (20 years) - From 4 years up to 24 years of age
- Surya Dasa (six years) - from 24 years to 30 years of age
- Chandra Dasa (ten years) - from 30 years to 40 years of age
- Mangala Dasa (seven years) - from 40 years to 47 years of age
- Rahu Dasa (18 years) - from 47 to 65 years of age
- Guru Dasa (16 years) - from 65 to 81 years of age

- Shani Dasa (19 years) - from 81 to 100 years of age

Vimshottari Dasa affects the lifetime of a native as follows:

- During childhood - parents and the health of natives
- During adolescence or teenage - education
- During youth - mind, job, and family
- During old age - health, children, and caretaker of the native

For the above example, Ketu Dasa happened until he or she was 4 years old. Ketu was in the house of Shukra in Kendra, which represents father. Hence, this child's birth was good in terms of his or her health and the progress of the native's father.

From 4 years of age onwards, the native was influenced by Shukra Dasa. This period affects education. Shukra is in its own house, which is also the house of writing and artistic nature. The house of education is the fourth house occupied by Surya, Shani, and Rahu for this native. Rahu and Shani result in the child being thoughtful and introverted while Shani also renders interest in science. Buddha in the 5th house results in building the native's interesting in calculations. Therefore, the native would have likely been educated with a deep interest in science and mathematics.

From 24 to 30 years of age, Surya Dasa influenced this native. Surya, in this native's birth chart, is in the 4th house giving the individual the push needed to start his or her own business and earning a lot of fame at a young age. Chandra, the lord of the 12th house, brought luck and good fortune, resulting in good success in business for the native.

From 40 to 47 years, this native was influenced by Mangala Dasa. Even though Mars is a benefic planet, for this native, it is positioned in the 8th house, which results in a big setback to his profession and business.

Rahu Dasa for this person is the next. This planet is in debilitation but is in Kendra, and likely to have had good fortune. However, health problems could have come up during the Rahu Dasa for the native.

Guru Dasa sets in only at 62 years for this native, and it might be the best years of his or her life. The native is likely to lead a restful, serene life during Guru Dasa.

Transit of Planets

Usually, to study the transit of planets, only Shani, Guru, and Rahu are considered. This is because other planets move fast. Surya, Buddha, and Shukra rotate once a year, Mangala takes two years, Chandra takes just a month, and Ketu is always opposite to Rahu. So, it is enough to see only Shani (Saturn, which takes 30 years to complete one cycle), Rahu (which takes 18 years to complete one cycle), and Guru (which takes 12 years to complete one cycle) to study the transit of planets.

When a planet transits through the debilitation signs or the signs owned by its enemies, it will not give good, auspicious results. For example, when Saturn transits through Leo, Cancer, Scorpio, and Aries (also the sign of debilitation), which are owned by its enemies, it will combust and cannot reflect its full potential for about 25 days every year during the 19-year Mahadasha.

For Shukra, this inauspicious transits will happen when it passes through Cancer and Leo, both ruled by Venus' enemies. During its own mahadasha, it will combust once in a year for about 20 days. Also, these transits become very important during the Saturn-Venus sub-period of 2 years and 9 months.

When the owner of a Dasa or time period is in its sign of exaltation, its own sign, or in the signs of friendly planets, then the concerned Graha will give auspicious effects. In such circumstances, even during retrogressions, these planets do not give bad effects, and they could give auspicious effects.

For example, in Shani mahadasha, when Saturn transits through Capricorn, Aquarius, Virgo, Gemini, Libra, and Taurus, which are all exalted signs for the planet, then it will retrograde annually for about three to four months.

For Shukra mahadasha, this will happen when the planet transits through Gemini. Libra, Virgo, Aquarius, Pisces, and Capricorn. The duration of retrograde will be for about three to four months once a year.

Transits of planets are especially significant when they are in conjunction with the Moon. When Saturn crosses over the Moon, it is called *Sade Sati*. The native is likely to face big losses or progresses, depending on which sign the Moon is in. In the same way, Saturn passing through the 8th house from the Moon also results in tensions and losses.

In the above example, Guru crossed over Rahu/Shani when the native was 2, 14, 26, 28, 50, and 62 years of age. Saturn and Jupiter were in conjunction when the native was 12, 24, 36, 48, and 60 years of age. At the time of these transits, Jupiter was over the 4th house over Shani and Rahu, resulting in a change of residence or purchase of a new property. When Jupiter transited over the 7th house lorded by Saturn, then the native got married. Saturn over Saturn or Rahu resulted in losing business.

Also, the native experienced Sade Sati in 1968 and again in 1996. In 1968, the native lost academic interest, and in 1996, the native's mother fell ill, and there was a death in the family. Short transits show their results more prominently and effectively than mahadasha and antardashas. Yet, major transits affect the native in a big way. Shani transit over Chandra is very important. Guru and Rahu transiting through the Lagna and the Moon give equal results. Typically, superimposing Dasas over the transit of planets gives more accurate predictions than otherwise.

Besides the Vimshottari Dasha System, the Yogini Dasha System is also used to calculate Dasas and transits of planets. It is important to realize the extreme difficulty of making accurate predictions in Vedic Astrology. There are multiple factors to be considered, each of which has its own rules and regulations for computations and mathematical analysis.

Dasas, transits of planets, divisional charts, planetary strengths, avasthas, and many more determinants are to be considered before accurate predictions can be arrived at. Even helped by computational software, the process of predictions for just one native can take a few hours, or perhaps, more.

Chapter 12: Ashtakavarga: Destiny Dots at a Glance

This final chapter in this of Vedic Astrology deals with Ashtakavarga or the eight-fold point system used to make predictions by just glancing at a horoscope. Although this tool is an independent subject, using it with the other tools mentioned in the previous chapters of this book can be a powerful predictive approach. Let us look at how this technique helps.

Sage Parashara also mentions the significance of this technique, used not only to determine the beneficial effects of planets through the Chandra and the ascendant but also to discover the auspiciousness of the houses by studying the transits of planets. The Ashtakavarga technique employs Bindu (dots) and Rekha (lines) to determine planets' position. This powerful tool is considered while analyzing mahadashas and antardashas of planets.

The Ashtakavarga table has multiple rows and columns. The top row is for the 12 Zodiac signs from Aries up to Pisces. The first right column is the ascendant's degree, and the first left column has the seven planets. Rahu and Ketu do not feature in the Ashtakavarga table. Instead, the Lagna itself is treated as a complete planet. The row against each planet represents the planet's score in the Zodiac sign of the respective column head. The last row is the combined score of each sign regarding the eight planets (including the Lagna). The last column is the combined score of each planet regarding the 12 signs.

In the Ashtakavarga table, the score of each planet-Zodiac sign combination varies from 0 to 8. Each planet's total score regarding the 12 Zodiac signs can range from 0 to 56. Only rules must interpret any Ashtakavarga table. Here are the two rules:

Rule #1 - Look at the row of each planet. You will notice that for every one of the 12 signs, the planet under consideration gets a score running from 0 to 8. Each point is an indicator of the planet's power to influence the sign related to the score. Here are the sub-rules related to Rule #1:

- If the planet is in a sign where its score is between five and eight, then the planet will give auspicious results.

- If the planet-sign combination score is four, then the results will be average.

- If the planet-sign score is between zero and three, then it will give inauspicious results.

Rule #2 - Next, look at the individual sign totals, which is the last row of the table. The values in this row will range from 0 to 56. This row represents the power of each Zodiac sign to give related to its relationship with the planet position. Follow these guidelines to interpret the numerical values of this last row:

- A Zodiac sign with a score of over 30 typically gives good results.

- A sign with a total score of less than 25 means it is inauspicious.

- Signs with scores between 25 and 80 give average results.

The following information can be obtained from an Ashtakavarga table:

- Weakest house - that house that has the lowest score
- Weak houses - those that have less than 25 points
- Average houses - those with a score between 25 and 30
- Strong houses - those with the highest scores or above 30

It is also important to know what the total score of all the 12 signs put together should be 337. If this number is different, then something has gone wrong in the table. Recheck it before moving on and trying to interpret it.

How to Use the Ashtakavarga Table for Rashi Chart Interpretation

First, mark the Lagna. Then mark the lowest and highest numerical value in the chart. Note down the house and Rashis these two numbers correspond to. Suppose the lowest number is in the 5th house, then start your analysis by investigating the 5th house, which primarily deals with children. While a problem with adolescents is indicated, it need not be a significant issue. The lowest number is only an indication for you or your astrologer to conduct a more detailed investigation in that particular house. As you dig deep, the depth and significance of the problem will become clear.

Similarly, if the lowest score is in the 9th house, it makes sense to investigate there. The 9th house deals with several important aspects of a native's life. But the most important factor of the 9th house is about the father or the head of the family. So, a low score here could mean that the native's father may have died at an early age or had health issues.

Another relevant point to note about Ashtakavarga charts is that they should not be used by themselves or separately to make predictions. It is critical to check other astrology factors, including the pertinent divisional charts, planetary strengths, etc. to interpret a native's life and life experiences correctly. But this table can be a powerful indicator of where to begin the investigation and find answers to other questions likely to arise as you verify various angles of a native's horoscope.

Here are more points about the Ashtakavarga table that will help you make good predictions:

If the number in the first house or Lagna is low and is also less than 25, then it means the native needs other people's support to do his or her work. This individual cannot do his or her karma by himself or herself. Such individuals always need somebody with them and cannot survive without a partner.

If the first house has a high score, then such people enjoy working alone. Such individuals are likely to have high egos, although they can make correct decisions with little help from others. People with a high score in the Lagna generally succeed, provided the other planetary positions are promising.

If the 12th house score is low, such individuals also have a good life because opportunities for loss and suffering are likely to be few. If the 12th score is the lowest, then such individuals are misers. They either don't have the mindset or the opportunity to spend money.

If the score of your 11th house (house of gains) is greater than that of your 12th house (house of loss), then too, it is good because it means you will gain more than you lose. If the condition is reversed, that is to say, the score in your 12th house is greater than that of your 11th house, then you are likely to spend more than you gain or earn.

Case Study of Ashtakavarga Table Scores

Let us take these scores of an Ashtakavarga table:

1st house - 25, 2nd house - 28, 3rd house - 33, 4th house - 29, 5th house - 26, 6th house - 24, 7th house - 35, 8th house - 35, 9th house - 26, 10th house - 27, 11th house - 22, and 12th house - 27. If you notice, the total score is 337. Let's interpret these scores:

- The average score is 337/12 = 28, which is also taken as a threshold. So, less than 28 is a bad score, and over 28 is a good score. This is the reason 25 to 30 is taken as average scores.

- In the above case study, the 1st, 5th, 6th, 9th, 10th, 11th, and 12th houses have scored less than 28. The 3rd, 4th, 7th, and 8th houses are of good value. The 2nd house with a value of 28 is average.

- Any house with a score of less than 25 is bad. Here, the 9th and the 11th houses are quite bad, the 11th being very bad. Values of the 1st, 9th, 10th, and 11th houses are also less than 30, which means they are negative indicators.

- The Lagna and the 4th houses also have less than 30.

- The value of 25 in the 1st house means that the native will boost his or her life after 25 years of age.

- The value of the 2nd house is 28, which is greater than the 11th and 12th houses' values. This means that the native will not waste their earnings and money.

- But the value of his 12th house is greater than the value of his 11th house, which means the native cannot hold on to his savings/earnings. This person's expenditure will be more than his or her income/earnings/savings.

Houses 1, 5, and 9 represent Bandhu, and the total for this native is 77

Houses 2, 6, and 10 represent Sevaka, and the total is 79

Houses 3, 7, and 11 represent Poshaka; the total value is 90

Houses 4, 8, and 12 represent Ghataka; the total value is 91

If the Bandhu group has the highest tally, then the native will have ample resources, will do good karma, and be charitable. If the Sevaka group has the highest tally, then the native will be in employment or service, and he or she will be money-minded. If the Poshaka group gets the highest tally, then the native may be an industrialist, employer, or a boss. If the Ghataka group has the highest tally, then the native could be very poor.

It takes time and effort to understand and interpret the Ashtakavarga table. But, when used with the other astrological tools and techniques mentioned in this book, it can be a powerfully accurate predictor of horoscopes.

Conclusion

At first glance, Vedic Astrology might appear confounding to the novice. It is easy to relate to this feeling of being overwhelmed by the information this engrossing and captivating subject covers. Yes, it does take a bit of effort on your part to understand the concepts of Jyotishya.

But you can rest assured that your efforts will not be in vain. With sustained and persistent practice and reading, you will learn to look at a horoscope or table, use quick computations, and gauge what lies in store for the native.

Knowing Jyotishya is useful for your own life. When you achieve great success, you can review your own horoscope and know that you are not doing this on your own. You will learn that your past karmas are giving you beneficial outcomes. When you suffer a lot, again, simply reading your horoscope will give you an insight as to how long you must endure the difficult times.

Viewing the happy and sad parts of your life with equanimity will keep you grounded and empower you to give your best shot to everything you try. For such individuals, successes will far outnumber the failures. So, go ahead, and read the book again and again until you have mastered the basics. You can then move on to advanced levels.

Here's another book by Mari Silva that you might like

Your Free Gift (only available for a limited time)

Thanks for getting this book! If you want to learn more about various spirituality topics, then join Mari Silva's community and get a free guided meditation MP3 for awakening your third eye. This guided meditation mp3 is designed to open and strengthen ones third eye so you can experience a higher state of consciousness. Simply visit the link below the image to get started.

https://spiritualityspot.com/meditation

Resources

https://yogadigest.com/introduction-vedic-astrology/

https://www.astroguruonline.com/books-ancient-astrology/

https://www.speakingtree.in/blog/the-types-of-vedic-astrology

https://www.astrojyoti.com/9planets.htm

https://www.astrology-prophets.com/9-planets.php

http://www.theartofvedicastrology.com/?page_id=117

https://astrosurkhiyan.blogspot.com/2014/06/planetary-friendships.html

https://ommrudraksha.com/planet-friends-friends-and-enemies-friendship-chart-astrology

https://vicdicara.wordpress.com/2010/06/04/determining-planetary-friendship-and-enmity/

https://www.appliedvedicastrology.com/2019/08/31/the-real-meaning-of-planetary-aspects-the-nature-of-desire-in-our-chart-part-1/

http://www.theartofvedicastrology.com/?page_id=146

http://www.vaastuinternational.com/astrology4.html

https://jyotishvidya.com/bhavatbhavam.htm

http://www.bhairavastrology.com/expertise/vedic-astrology/

https://astrobix.com/astrosight/564-ayanamsa-meaning-ayanamsa.html

https://www.youtube.com/watch?v=E2AWLDwolVo

https://www.astrojyoti.com/lesson9.htm

http://www.bhairavastrology.com/expertise/vedic-astrology/

https://www.youtube.com/watch?v=NNkV9sWPVtk

http://www.theartofvedicastrology.com/?page_id=127

https://www.youtube.com/watch?v=00-PlzTA5ZQ

https://www.heerejawharat.com/astrology/astrology.php

https://www.astrojyoti.com/lesson1.htm

https://astrologer-astrology.com/zodiac_lord_indian_vedic_astrology_jyotish.htm

https://blog.indianastrologysoftware.com/study-of-divisional-charts/

http://www.theartofvedicastrology.com/?page_id=430

https://srath.com/principles-of-divisional-charts/

https://www.linkedin.com/pulse/importance-divisional-charts-vedic-astrology-pt-b-p-upadhyay

http://www.theartofvedicastrology.com/?page_id=458

https://www.dirah.org/shadbala.htm

https://vedicastroadvice.com/articles-on-vedic-astrology/shadbala_and_vedic_astrology/

https://medium.com/thoughts-on-jyotish/shadbala-the-6-sources-of-strength-4c5befc0c59a

https://www.speakingtree.in/blog/art-of-prediction-part-iii-dashas-and-transits

https://www.futurepointindia.com/article/en/timing-of-event-through-dasa-and-transit-8799

https://psychologicallyastrology.com/2019/12/23/fine-tuning-predictions-dasha-plus-transit/

https://vedicsiddhanta.in/2016/11/power-of-vimsotri-dasha-how-transits.html#.Xz1cTvlKh0w

https://astrobix.com/learn/359-determination-of-results-through-ashtakvarga.html

https://sreenivasdesabhatla.wordpress.com/2013/05/18/ashtakavarga-system-of-prediction-1/

https://www.youtube.com/watch?v=khqRo4Ujw0M

https://psychologicallyastrology.com/2019/10/12/ashtakvarga-practical-ways-of-using-the-tables/

http://circleof360.blogspot.com/2018/08/understaning-ashtakvarga-table-with.html